This book covers the investment insights, the mistakes, the lessons learned, and the wisdom observed over our combined 60 years of experience. We hope you find it informative and helpful.

Sincerely,

Selwyn and Jonathan Gerber

RVWWEALTH

Financial Planning • Investments

310.945.4000 • RVWWealth.com

THE WEALTH BLUE PRINT

BUILD LONG TERM WEALTH AND AVOID THE WALL STREET TRAPS

WHAT TO DO AND WHY IT WORKS

SELWYN GERBER, CPA

WITH

JONATHAN L. GERBER, CPA, MBT, PFS

ADAM SMITH PUBLISHING COMPANY

The Wealth Blue Print

ISBN 978-0-692-92629-1

Adam Smith Publishing Company
19 Essex Place
Memphis, TN 38120-2422

*To the financial planners, stockbrokers, and
wealth advisors I have met over many decades
who, unknowingly, showed me the light.*

-Selwyn

*To our colleagues at RVW who have supported
us with diligence and patience while working on
this book, and for their continued focus on, and
commitment to the long-term financial wellbeing
of each of our clients every day.*

-Jonathan

Contents

Appendix (Cont.)

Preface

In 1977, the price level for the Dow Jones Industrial Average stood at roughly 850. By mid-2017 it had risen to over 20,000—a twentyfold increase. After factoring in dividends (assuming they were reinvested) an investment made in 1977, when I immigrated to this great country, would have increased more than fortyfold!

During this period, from 1977 to 2017, the market* suffered some of the largest single-day losses ever (both in points and percentages), weathered the chaos following the 9/11 terrorist attacks (which shut down trading for the longest time period since FDR's death in 1945), the tech-bubble and endured several major global financial crises. Yet, each time those downturns eventually each worked like a compressed spring being released, propelling the market to new highs.

The jaw dropping 50% decline of 2008 was followed by a rapid upward march that put the market more than 40% above its pre-crash high by the end of 2016. If we include dividends, $100,000 invested at the pre-crisis peak would have grown to over $181,000 despite falling as low as $50,000 at the worst points of the downturn.

Sadly, many equity investors did not reap the benefits of those market rebounds simply because the ride was too turbulent, too gut-wrenching. They followed the headlines and doom-and-gloom reports by the pundits—and sold out at the worst time

---

* Throughout this book we will refer to "the market," which generally means the market for equities (i.e. stocks) as measured and represented by popular indexes such as the S&P 500® or the Dow Jones Industrial Average.

possible, while others were steadfast or were poised to take full advantage of these buying opportunities.

Until 12 years ago, my partners and I dutifully referred clients of our CPA firm to leading stockbrokers and wealth managers, believing that they had better tools, research and information than we could offer. But the results were almost always disappointing. We found that frequently the fancier and more impressive the marketing materials, the worse the performance.

> "The market, like the Lord, helps those who help themselves. But, unlike the Lord, the market does not forgive those who know not what they do."
> – Warren Buffett

CPA's tend to be the calm, steady, clear-eyed bunch in the financial world. Our work may be less thrilling than that of a trader plugged into a Bloomberg terminal, but there is a method, a system and logic behind all that we do. We understand financial statements, the impact of income taxes on returns and are by training bottom-line oriented.

And so, we decided to apply the accountant's perspective to the wealth management process. After decades of watching the "professionals" usually underperform and after reading countless books, articles, and Nobel Prize-winning papers, the optimal approach—what we call *Intellibeta Investing*—was born. *Intellibeta Investing* is an evidence-based approach to investing that recognizes the superiority of low-cost index funds (also known as "passive" investing) to high-cost actively managed funds (such as mutual funds, hedge funds, or any other investment vehicle that uses "active" investing). *Intellibeta Investing* further builds on the discoveries made by Nobel Prize-winner Eugene Fama and his associate Kenneth French in their now-famous Fama-French model (see sidebar "The Fama-French Three-Factor Model" on page 128). Their research showed that while broad market exposure has delivered stellar risk-adjusted returns over the long term, this performance can be enhanced by overweighting towards companies that exhibit specific attributes. For example, smaller companies tend to do better than larger ones and value (i.e. underpriced) stocks do better than growth stocks over time.

We decided to call our wealth management company RVW, reflecting the initials of Rip Van Winkle, acknowledging that for most investors, ignoring news headlines and market fluctuations was the optimal mindset—and that developing an attitude of indifference towards volatility while focusing on fundamentals and on one's long term financial plan was optimal. Indeed, the mythical Mr. Van Winkle would have been an ideal client of our firm.

If we can see further than most, it is because we proudly sit on the shoulders of giants such as Warren Buffett, Charlie Munger, Prof. Jeremy Siegel, Prof. Burton Malkiel and John Bogle all of whom have written extensively and persuasively about the power of investing in index funds, the fallibility of picking stocks, cost minimization and most importantly have had legendary investment success to prove their strategies. Now that we have been doing this for over 12 years, we also have our own first-hand experience and research to draw upon, enriching the "data set" still further.

This book was born from our desire to share and explain this approach. More specifically, it aims to show you how and why so-called "active" investing, whether done by you or someone else (your financial advisor, mutual fund manager or hedge fund manager) is for most, a losing game. You will learn how and why a portfolio of carefully selected index funds (when properly allocated across asset classes, with an allocation to bonds when needed, and a good dose of willpower to ignore day-to-day fluctuations) is the strategy most likely to deliver long term investment success.

Essentially, we seek to hoist the mast and set the sails so that the sailboat is propelled farthest by a given velocity of wind—and then we adjust the sails and make course-corrections from time to time. We recognize that although we don't control the wind, we can optimize the effect of a gust on our vessel's forward movement and minimize the headwinds of costs and taxes.

For those of you who wish to skim through the book, it is stuffed full of insightful quotes, figures, and sidebars. But for novices and veterans alike, we urge you to give some time and attention to the full book, or at least pick out some of the chapters where you think you might have room to improve your clarity on the issues. Chapters 1 through 5 focus on how and why even the best investors go wrong. Chapters 6 through 11 focus on how to do things right once we've ditched all the nonsense. The final chapter, Chapter 12, tells you how to put it altogether and make it a part of your life, both in thought and in action.

Uniquely, this book has a three-track approach:

1. The text provides a detailed description of why markets work as they do, and how to optimally participate in that upward movement;

2. The block quotes tell the story in pithy, useful statements conveying key principles; and

3. The charts, cartoons and illustrations provide a pictorial summary of all the key points.

I am proud that my son, Jonathan L. Gerber, CPA, PFP, MBT, a partner in our firm, has provided much valuable assistance in the research and writing of this book. He and the other RVW team members have together nurtured a collaborative environment and a culture of ongoing learning in which vigorous debate, an open mind and a total focus on the long term financial wellbeing of each client have built the firm into what is today. This democratic approach with egos parked firmly at the front door, has benefitted both us and our clients.

Jonathan and I hope that you'll absorb some of the perspective we've acquired through our research and experience in the art and science of the prudent stewardship of wealth. The anecdotes, common sense, and cold, hard data in this book can serve the reader as an anchor or touchstone. They will help tie you to reality, so you don't get swept up into the periodic bouts of euphoria and despondence that characterize market cycles. As Charlie Munger sagely observes, the optimal state of mind for the savvy investor is equanimity—that rare state of internal peace knowing that your financial well-being is intact and that your investment sailboat is on course.

Selwyn Gerber
Los Angeles, CA
July 2017

Chapter 1

Laziness Pays

"Rip Van Winkle would make the ideal stock market investor. Rip could invest in the market before his nap and when he woke up 20 years later, he'd be happy. He would have been asleep through all the ups and downs in between."

– Richard Thaler, Economist

"I am essentially a Rip Van Winkle investor."

– Warren Buffett

Most investors hurt themselves by doing too much. It is as if they live in a world that is the exact opposite of the one lived in by Irving Washington's protagonist in *Rip Van Winkle*. The *less* Rip works, the more his farm shrinks; yet the *more* we work, the more our nest egg suffers. Again and again we sacrifice our nest eggs on the altar of activity, seemingly unable to ignore the siren call of Wall Street.

Our excessive trading activity is not just fruitless. It's downright destructive! *Real* companies in the *real* economy, like Apple, Microsoft, and Boeing, are barely affected by the day-to-day fluctuations of the market. Sure, they can borrow at a lower rate or issue new shares at a higher price if their stock price is higher, but their employees do not change the work that they do from day to day just because the stock price ticked up or down a few points. But while business carries on as usual, we trade and trade and trade, generating endless fees for an army of financial middle men. The economy marches onward and upward while we hand a bigger and bigger piece of the "take" over to Wall Street. Why?

> "We would all be better investors if we just made fewer decisions."
>
> – Daniel Kahneman, Economist
> Nobel Laureate

If only we could be more like Rip Van Winkle and ignore all the headlines, chatter, and background noise, stay invested in quality equities without handing over all those fees, we would let our stocks provide the steady, long-term gains they deliver so beautifully over time, uninterrupted. Investment success, it seems, comes not from the triumph of action over inaction, but the triumph of inaction over action. Or, more specifically, the triumph of *disciplined* inaction over *impulsive* action.

> "Don't confuse motion and progress. A rocking horse keeps moving but does not make any progress."
>
> – Alfred A. Montapert, Author
> *The Supreme Philosophy of Man*

Bulls, Bears, and Other Hairy Creatures

It's easy to see why we get skittish and are tempted to act on impulse—after all, it's a jungle out there. It's the classic battle of the bears, bulls, and pigs. On the one hand, the frenzy might excite us to jump into the action, and on the other, we might be scared off from stocks entirely. And since there are no limits to what the market can do in the short-run, the daily outcomes are anyone's guess. Caught up in a euphoric frenzy, we tend to buy high, and later in the doldrums of market despair, we sell low.

Mr. Market

Warren Buffett's mentor, Benjamin Graham, came up with an insightful way to think about the market's short-term erratic behavior: He told investors that they should think of the market as a manic-depressive mythical person by the name of "Mr. Market," and further, that by virtue of trading in the same market as Mr. Market, they were effectively in the position of co-owning a business in partnership with Mr. Market.

Some days your partner, Mr. Market, shows up at the office in one of his depressive states. He's down in the dumps, and in such terrible shape that, to him, even the lines at the grocery store look like proof that the world is coming undone. In desperation, he offers to sell you his share in the business at a deep discount. Then, the next day he shows up again in one of his manic (euphoric) states and can see nothing but clear skies and sunshine ahead. Beaming from ear to ear, he pleads with you to buy your share of the business for an outrageously high price.

Warren Buffett still uses this analogy today, and urges investors to adopt it as their own framework for understanding the market's erratic behavior. *Although in the short term the mood swings of Mr. Market determine the value of one's portfolio, in the long run the profits earned by the businesses owned are the real determinant of true value.*

Perhaps we might tell ourselves that if we were just omniscient, if we just had perfect foresight, *then* we could master our emotions. In the certainty of our perfect knowledge we could act with calm, unaffected by the chaos of the jungle, and knowing precisely when to get in and when to get out. But here's the thing: No one is omniscient, *and* no amount of hard work will get you there, or even close! This is because the short-term forces that drive the daily ups and down of the market (what Keynes called "animal spirits") are of a nature that simply can't be predicted. When you pit these "animal spirits" against each other, the outcome is simply unpredictable. As soon as the bears take control, the market can flip and go the other way. And, who knows? Maybe once the bulls are on top there will be a glitch in the system and we'll get a monster drop like the May 6, 2010 "Flash Crash" that caused the market to plunge 9% and bounce back in a single day.

> "In a bull market, you're not as smart as you think you are — and in a bear market, you're not as dumb as you think you are."
>
> – Ben Carlson, CFA, Director of Institutional Asset Management at Ritholtz Wealth Management

Goodbye to the Jungle

If, on the other hand, we step out of the jungle and into a helicopter, we can begin to see the bigger, more important picture shown in Figures 1-1 and 1-2. Business activity (and even life itself) seems to have a way of multiplying itself such that each failure becomes a nutrient, a lesson, or a springboard from which new heights are reached. Just as trees fall in the jungle and become nutrient for a new generation of trees, the dotcom bubble laid vast networks for fiber-optic cables that became fertile soil for the likes of Google and Amazon. The overall growth in the stock market reflects this more fundamental, underlying activity. This is why, despite the short-term fluctuations (or the occasional falling tree) we see an ever upward march in the stock market.

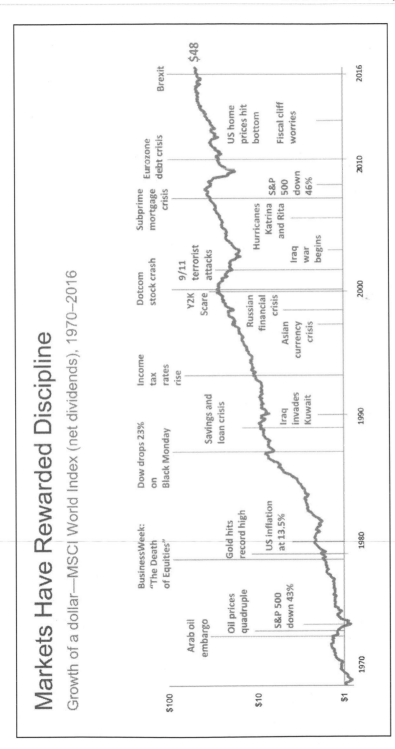

Figure 1-1: Despite a never-ending stream of "crises" the market has continued its long-term upward march. Source: Dimensional Fund Advisors.

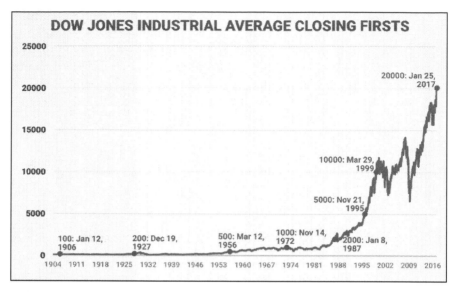

Figure 1-2: The stock market has risen steadily over time, going back for more than a century.

Over the short term there will be bear markets from time to time, but the long-term history of equity investing indicates that we can ignore the predictions of recessions, depressions, and runaway inflation—not because they won't happen, but because they won't matter. Similarly, individual stocks may sizzle and fizzle, but the market aggregate will continue its long-term upward march.

> "The fundamental impulse that sets and keeps the capitalist engine in motion comes from the new consumers, goods, the new methods of production . . . that incessantly revolutionize the economic structure from within . . . destroying the old one . . . creating a new one. This process of Creative Destruction is the essential fact about capitalism."
>
> – Joseph Schumpeter, Economist
> *Capitalism, Socialism and Democracy*

Bear Markets Always End

But what about a truly big, bad bear market? Perhaps you're afraid of one so bad that you couldn't even trust yourself to stay calm and do the right thing.

Bear markets are nothing to fear. They have happened before and they will happen again. They are a normal and necessary part of the markets' circle-of-life. Events like the 1929 crash, the oil crisis of the 1970s, the 1989 savings and loan crisis, Long-term Capital Management's bailout in 1998, the "dot.com" crash of 2000, the 9/11 attacks in 2001, and the 2008/2009 banking and real estate crisis each had an immediate impact. And yet each time the market bounced back and resumed its steady movement onward and upward (Figure 1-1). *History is solidly on the side of the bulls.*

> "This is the third time Warren [Buffett] and I have seen our holdings in Berkshire Hathaway go down, top tick to bottom tick, by 50% . . . [I]f you're not willing to react with equanimity to a market price decline . . . you're not fit to be a common shareholder . . ."
>
> – Charlie Munger, Vice Chairman
> Berkshire Hathaway

Market-Timing Doesn't Work

Short-term declines are a fact of life for investors. In order to benefit from the bigger, longer-term gains that more than compensate for the losses, investors need to be able and willing to weather the declines. It's important to stay the course and hang on during tough times because most of the strong, upward thrusts of the stock market happen in surprisingly short intervals, and we can't predict exactly when these upward bursts will happen. In fact, nearly all of the market's total return from 1926 to 2017 took place in just 49 months. That's just over four years' worth of trading days over a 91-year period—*a mere 4% of the trading days*. In 2016 alone, the total gain of 11.96% came from just five of the best trading days. To be successful at timing the market, two decisions must be made correctly: When to get in and when to get out (in either order). The chances of getting *both* right is very small.

> "If I have noticed anything over these 60 years on Wall Street, it is that people do not succeed in forecasting what's going to happen to the stock market."
>
> — Benjamin Graham,
> Mentor to Warren Buffett

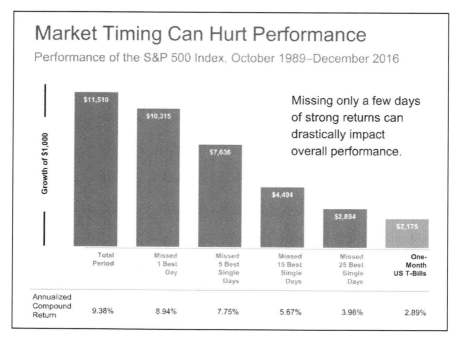

Figure 1-3: Missing just a handful of the best trading days can dramatically reduce returns. Source: Dimensional Fund Advisors and RVW Research.

The History of Bear and Bull Markets, 1926—2017

BEAR	Bear Dates	Bull Dates	BULL
34 Months	Sep 1929 - June 1932	Jul 1932 - Jan 1945	151 Months
6 Months	Jun 1946 - Nov 1946	Dec 1946 - Oct 1949	35 Months
7 Months	Aug 1956 - Feb 1957	Mar 1957 - July 1957	5 Months
5 Months	Aug 1957 - Dec 1957	Jan 1958 - Jul 1958	7 Months
6 Months	Jan 1962 - June 1962	Jul 1962 - Apr 1963	10 Months
8 Months	Feb 1966 - Sep 1966	Oct 1966 - Mar 1967	6 Months
19 Months	Dec 1968 - June 1970	Jul 1970 - Mar 1971	9 Months
21 Months	Jan 1973 - Sep 1974	Oct 1974 - Jun 1976	21 Months
14 Months	Jan 1977 - Feb 1978	Mar 1978 - Jul 1978	5 Months
20 Months	Dec 1980 - July 1982	Aug 1982 - Oct 1982	3 Months
3 Months	Sep 1987 - Nov 1987	Dec 1987 - May 1989	18 Months
5 Months	Jun 1990 - Oct 1990	Nov 1990 - Feb 1991	4 Months
2 Months	July 1998 - Aug 1998	Sep 1998 - Nov 1998	3 Months
25 Months	Sep 2000 - Sep 2002	Oct 2002 - Oct 2006	49 Months
16 Months	Nov 2007 - Feb 2009	Mar 2009 - Jul 2017	101 Months

Figure 1-4: From 1926 to mid-2017, the market spent nearly twice as much time in bull markets (427 months) as it did in bear markets (191 months). *It's not timing the market, but time in the market that counts.* Source: RVW Research.

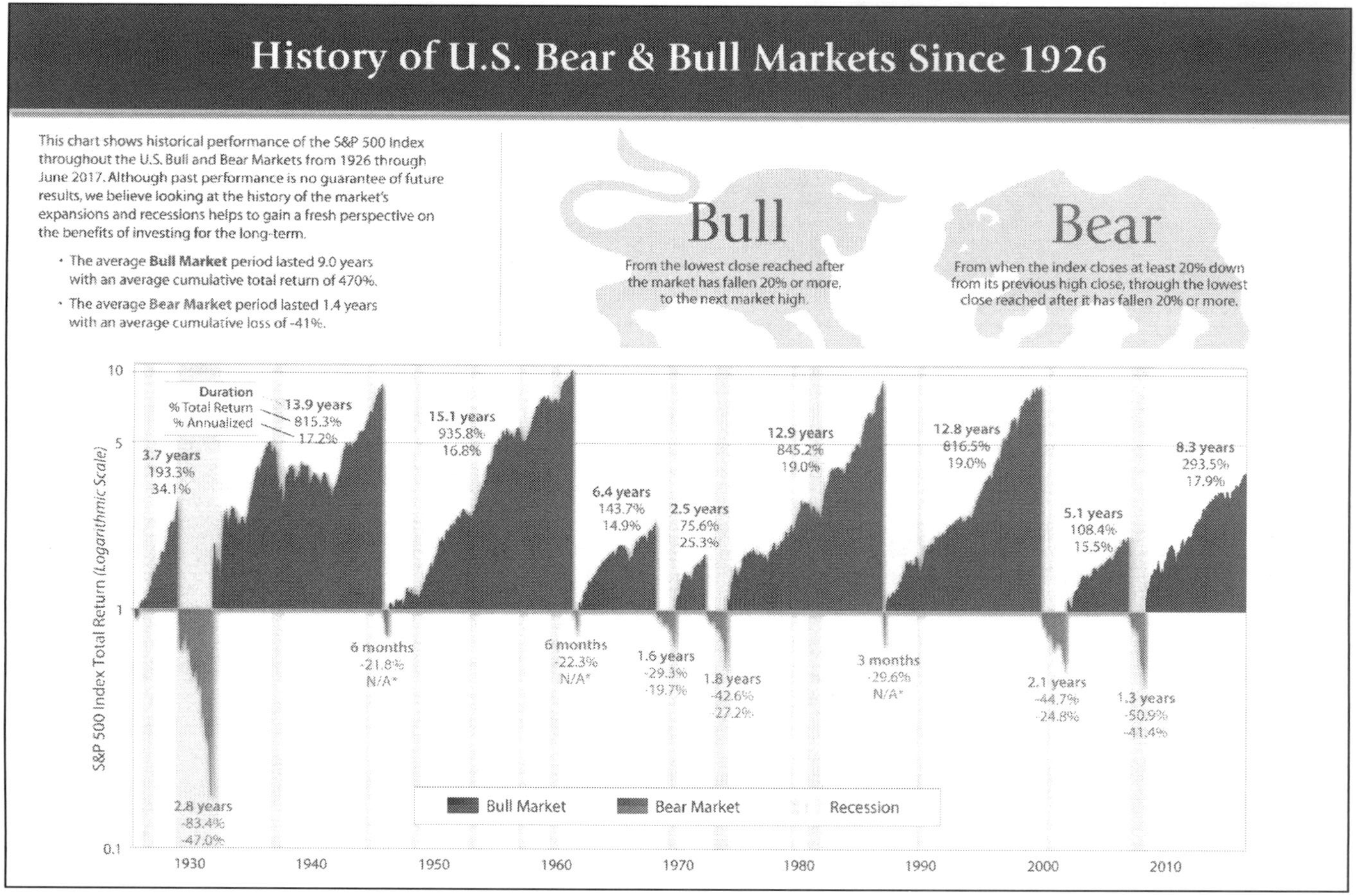

Figure 1-5: Another way to see the same information in Figure 1-4. Source: First Trust Advisors, L.P., Morningstar.

> It's not *timing* the market. It's *time in* the market.

Those who try to time the market often miss out on these upward thrusts. And given how important these are to the long-term returns of the market, missing out on these is a high price to pay for whatever short-term relief market timers get by sitting on the sidelines during market downturns. The only way to guarantee that you'll capture the full benefit of these strong but brief upward spurts is to hang on through both the ups and the downs.

Mark Hulbert, editor of the *Hulbert Financial Digest*, validated this point after he reviewed the performance of thirty-two market-timing newsletters over a ten-year period and found that not a single one had beaten the S&P 500®.

> "Santayana is right: History repeats and repeats, and forget it at your peril. All bubbles break, all investment frenzies pass away. You absolutely must ignore the vested interests of the industry and the inevitable cheerleaders. The market is gloriously inefficient and wanders far from fair price but eventually, after breaking your heart and your patience, it will go back to fair value. Your task is to survive until that happens."
>
> – Jeremy Grantham, Co-Founder
> Grantham, Mayo, & Van Otterloo

Stock Picking Doesn't Work

Another form of active management is stock picking. This is where we place our trust in someone's ability (possibly our own) to pick individual stocks, loading up on the winners and avoiding the losers. The problem with this approach is that studies have shown again and again that even the best managers can't pull this off consistently and reliably. As far back as 1967, in a paper titled "The Performance of Mutual Funds in the Period 1945-1964," Nobel Prize-winning economist Michael C. Jensen demonstrated that, after taking fees into account, more than 80% of stock-picking mutual fund managers underperform. Since Jensen's initial insight, more and more studies have continued to validate the same basic conclusion: stock-picking mutual fund managers simply fail to consistently keep up with their benchmarks. These benchmarks are known as indexes, and will be covered in depth in Chapter 7. All you need to know for now is that there is a way to participate in the entire market or sectors of the market through specialized funds called index funds (which will be covered in Chapter 8). Doing so will save you from the costly blunders that usually come with all that activity.

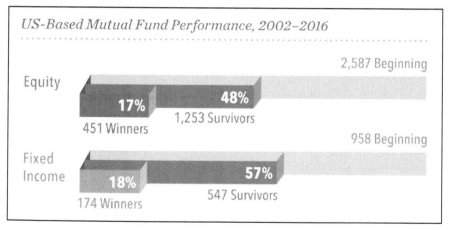

Figure 1-6: Out of 2,587 equity mutual funds, only 1,253 (48%) survived from 2002 to 2016. Of these 1,253 survivors, only 451 (17%) beat their benchmarks. The numbers are equally striking for fixed income mutual funds. Source: Dimensional Fund Advisors.

The stock market pricing system reflects all information known and knowable about what the fair price for a stock is at any particular moment in time. Despite this, stock pickers hold on to the belief that they can spot mispricings in the market, and that they have superior knowledge of the relevant factors compared to everyone else.

> *Individual stock-picking is like looking for a needle in a haystack. You can rummage through the haystack and risk losing the needle, or you can buy the whole haystack and know you've got it. Broadly diversified portfolios are the haystack.*

Tax and Cost Savings

You might be wondering how over 80% of active managers could underperform the indexes. After all, the indexes are like a thermometer that measures the average performance of the market, which itself is just the sum of all the traders, fund managers, and their accounts. So how could 80% be below the average? That's like a college saying 80% of its graduates are above the class average. It just doesn't make sense.

But this is where costs, fees, and taxes come in. This is where the financial and government sectors get their "takes". If there were no taxes, fees, or commissions from active management, then yes, about half of active managers would do better than the indexes and about half would do worse. But factor in all these costs, and the whole pack of active managers gets dragged down in a major way.

Horse Racing Sumo Wrestlers

Imagine two different horse races. In the first race, the riders are light-weight jockeys. In the second, the jockeys are replaced with sumo wrestlers. In the first race the average time will be quite fast. But in the second, even though the horses are the same, it will be a miracle for any of the horses to beat the average time from the first race. This is what it's like for active fund managers. Even the best struggle to beat low-cost index funds because of the sumo wrestler weight of taxes, fees, and commissions that they carry.

> "Index funds are like horses with 20-pound jockeys running against ones carrying 200-pound jockeys."
>
> – Andrew Tobias, Author

The costs that go hand-in-hand with active management are primarily management fees, transaction costs/commissions, and increased taxes, many of which are buried deep under the net asset value calculations and in the fine print. Your broker gets his or her office, pension, health insurance, and often cruises paid for by those extra fees and incentives.

> "It is high time for broader industry acknowledgment that passive management is a preferable default for most individual investors, and that active management should come with a brighter warning sticker of sorts."
>
> – Tom Tabile, Writer
> *Financial Times*

Mutual fund managers want to be paid handsomely, and the better or the more advanced their research or gadgetry, the more they will demand, which in turn offsets part of any benefit to investors. Since they are being paid to *do* something, they tend towards more activity and engage in many transactions throughout the year, each of which involves fees and commissions they pay to their brokers. On top of this, any profits they make on these trades are taxed when earned, meaning they'll generally be subject to the higher ordinary income tax rates. In contrast, a low-cost index fund doesn't bear these costs because no one is being paid for the sake of activity and there are far fewer transactions, which means transaction costs are low and most gains will be taxed at the far lower, long-term, capital gains tax rates.

We shouldn't forget, either, the effects of compounding. As the fees, costs, and taxes from active management constantly nibble away, year after year, at the gains we have, they cut into our ability to compound those gains. Giving up 2% per year (or more) might not sound like much, but if we do it every year for ten years, the effects are much more than just 2% of the total outcome.

> "The miracle of compounding returns is overwhelmed by the tyranny of compounding costs."
>
> – John C. Bogle, Founder
> The Vanguard Group

A Dynamic, Self-Selecting Group of Winners

It's fair to ask how a passive approach like investing in low-cost index funds could work at all. It defies common sense. How could passivity be productive at all? Like Rip Van Winkle, if we don't labor over the farm, shouldn't it shrink?

But the problem with this line of reasoning is that it's too narrowly focused. We need to zoom out and keep the full context in view. Just as industry and life tends to expand itself, so too do the fruits of tethering ourselves to that process. Even in the case of Rip Van Winkle, when he returns from his slumber the town has grown so much that he can barely recognize it. If he could have invested in a passive index fund representing the growing economic prosperity of his hometown, he would have returned indeed as a rich man.

Index funds allow us to ride the wave of this organic, economic process through a naturalistic self-selection process. As certain companies fade away (and long before they ever go bankrupt) they are removed from the indexes, and as other companies grow and expand, they join the indexes. All the while, the overall economy grows and grows and grows, powered by the innovation and energy of the free-market, capitalist system.

I, Pencil

In a brilliant essay, "I, Pencil", Leonard Read explains (from the perspective of a pencil) just how complex the processes are and how global the coordination is that goes into making something so simple as a pencil. *Because the essay is so powerful, we have included the full text in the appendix on page 203.*

To illustrate this point, of the original thirty companies included in the Dow Jones Industrial Average (DJIA) in 1926, only three have survived to today in their original form. Yet despite there being so many fallen trees, the dynamic, self-selecting process of the indexes has given us the results we see in Figure 1-1, ensuring that we can both "see the forest for the trees" *and* benefit from the forest without relying excessively on any one tree. The merits of this approach only increase with time, as in these rapidly changing times it becomes ever more difficult to identify which companies— if any—will survive into the future. In one way, we can think of this as merely a matter of diversification, which is fine, because diversification is indeed a cornerstone of any sound investment strategy. *But it's also more than that. It's not merely that you own a smattering of many different companies, but also that through the organic, self-selecting process of index funds, you end up owning more of the best-in-breed companies in their healthiest, thriving years, and less of the lesser companies as they fade out of existence.*

Junk Bonds May Offer Little Protection

Going back to the late 1970s and early 1980s, junk bonds, also known as "high-yield bonds", have been thought of as a high-return alternative to regular bonds but with the same basic risk protection of bonds as compared to stocks. The 2008 financial crisis shows just how misleading this idea can be. For the three worst months of the crisis, the performance of the S&P 500® and the JNK junk bonds ETF were almost indistinguishable, as shown in Figure 1-7.

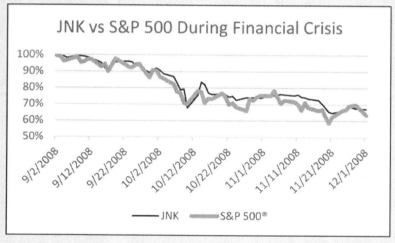

Figure 1-7: During the three worst months of the 2008 financial crisis, "junk bonds" or "high-yield bonds" performed just as poorly as stocks. *Source: RVW Research.*

Chapter 2

Hard Work Hurts

"[I]t was of no use to work on his farm; it was the most pestilent little piece of ground in the whole country; everything about it went wrong, and would go wrong, in spite of him."

– Washington Irving, Author
Rip Van Winkle

While we touched on why active investing generally doesn't pay, we must emphasize why hard work itself (whether done by a mutual fund manager or yourself) doesn't pay either—in fact, it hurts. Far too many investors try to pick stocks and time the market to their own detriment. We fool ourselves into thinking that, despite the odds and challenge we face, *we* will be the exception.

This is all good and fine if done for your own amusement— after all, there can be some amount of non-financial value we get out of the process, like what someone else might get from Las Vegas, Sudoku or chess. But if anyone, *anyone* other than yourself depends on, or will depend on, the results of your investment decisions, then we urge you to consider the challenges you face and the collateral damage that, more likely than not, will ensue.

Respect the Problem

The first step towards tackling any problem is to *respect* the problem. If you think it's easier than it is, you'll underestimate what you'll need (knowledge, skills, and software) and you'll dive in with fatal blind spots. What's worse, you might spend hours and hours trying to solve a problem that's inherently *unsolvable*.

> "Stock market forecasting is the attempt to predict the unknowable by measuring the irrelevant; a task that, in one way or another, profitably employs most people on Wall Street."
>
> – Jason Zweig, Columnist, *Wall Street Journal*
> "The Intelligent Investor"

Market-Timing

It's no exaggeration to say that predicting the short-term market is perhaps the most difficult of all problems to solve. Consider, for instance, just how hard it is to predict the weather more than a week into the future in many parts of the world. Then, replace all of those air molecules with individual people, hustling and bustling about in all the ways they influence the stock market. In the case of the weather, if there's a pressure drop in one area, the molecules have no choice but to move in that direction. The molecules cannot say, "I defy you, pressure! I will go my own way!" Yet human beings have this capacity (and often use it!). And, while it's true that, on average and overtime, the results in the economy do tend to follow the laws of economics, the moment-to-moment and even month-to-month changes are anyone's guess.

Weather vs. Climate

The day-to-day weather and the day-to-day movements of the stock market both get a lot of news coverage. But in both cases, what happens in a single day is of little consequence. If it rains, we might need an umbrella or we might get wet, but life goes on. What *really* matters—and what can change our lives in a meaningful way—is the long-term picture. If there's a change in *climate* (as opposed to *weather*) we'll need much more than an umbrella (our whole neighborhood may be flooded). Likewise, with investing, the day-to-day clamor means little, and our focus should instead be on the more impactful trends overtime. *For the astute investor, it's the climate rather than the weather than counts.*

For a more complete development of this powerful analogy, see the *Weather vs. Climate* article included in the appendix (p. 197).

Consider, also, the complex layers of human behavior involved. First, at the bottom of the pyramid, you have the consumers that buy the products and services of a company. Then, you have the employees and the management of the company. These two layers determine the fundamental, long-term prospects for the company. But in the short-run, you also have to consider a third layer—how investors will react to what they hear from the company or other sources. So, is this really a solvable problem? Can we really predict how everyone will react—which would require predicting both macro-level news on the economy and in the political sphere and micro-level news, and how all that news will be received. Short-term market behavior is simply not predictable.

> Don't believe the doom-and-gloomers. Even a broken clock gets it right twice a day.

Despite the reality of these challenges, many investors still believe it is within their power to buy stocks low and sell them high. This impression is nurtured by the stories they read about master traders who have successfully parlayed modest initial capital into billions of dollars. They believe that, if only they could learn the "secrets" to successful trading or market timing, they, too, could partake in this bottomless reservoir of potential wealth.

A simple math problem shows why this is such a tempting belief to hang on to: Nobel Prize-winning economist Robert Merton looked at what would happen if someone had perfectly predicted the direction the market would go in a given month at the beginning of that month and invested accordingly. With this seemingly simple strategy (and perfect accuracy) an investor starting in 1927 with only $1,000 would have earned more than $5.3 billion by 1978, making the $67,500 a buy-and-hold investor would have earned look like a pitiable sum. The return from this seemingly simple approach would have been an astonishing 35% annual return.

The incredible results from this simple experiment should make us suspicious. If anyone could turn $1,000 into $5.3 billion by simply predicting which way the market would go each month (up or down), then why isn't everyone doing this? Because, as we've already indicated, it's impossible to do. While the task is simple *to describe* ("Decide whether the market will go up or down each month."), the underlying clockwork that determines the outcome (whether the market will go up or down each month) is infinitely complex.

> Most investors seeking active management confuse stars with comets. The former shine forever; the latter crash and burn. But for a brief time, they both look identical.

Despite the impossibility of everyone making it rich through "sure-fire" systems and strategies, a veritable cottage industry has sprung up of so-called trading and market-timing gurus hawking trading systems and market-timing newsletters that promise investors outsized returns. Of course, if these peddlers really did know the secrets to the market's mysteries, they'd be spending their time using these strategies to make billions for themselves instead of selling subscriptions for $99.99 in late night infomercials.

The results from trading systems are often much worse than newsletters. Purchasers of these systems rarely know the risks involved or have realistic expectations for their potential profits. Moreover, once transaction costs and taxes are added into the equation, these strategies become even more unattractive.

Professional traders and market-timers are, in the end, hardly different from professional gamblers. Their "tips" and "insights" are the same kind of "sure thing" tip you'd get from a horse racing "report" sold to bettors at the track. Not surprisingly, very few join the ranks of the *uber*-wealthy, while the others eventually crash and burn, losing everything in the process.

The amateur traders, unfortunately, fare no better. Awed by

the lucky few, they pursue this path with a feverish zeal, only to find themselves holding an empty bag. The saddest part is that, like a casino, all of their losses go to "the house", only here, instead of building more casinos on the strip, their losses go to building the towering skyscrapers of Wall Street.

The Folly of Trusting Newsletters

In 1996, a group of business professors collaborated on a detailed study of the performance of investment newsletters. The study included 15,000 recommendations from 237 different newsletters between 1980 and 1992. Their conclusion: "There is no evidence that newsletters can time the market."

In addition, they discovered through their research that the average newsletter in the study lasted for less than four years. By the four-year mark, 95% of these supposed experts had stopped publishing.

Another market-timing skeptic, Mark Hulbert, publishes a service that tracks newsletter performance. He identified twenty-five newsletters that managed to stay in business during the ten-year period from 1988 to 1998, and found that these newsletters produced an average annual return of 11.1% — a full seven points below the S&P 500® average return of 18.1% over the same period.

Stock-Picking

It should be clear from the discussion above that attempting to ride stock market waves is no different from gambling. It is an unwise and inappropriate approach for anyone actually trying to benefit from their investing decisions. However, most investors, after quickly learning the follies of market-timing, nevertheless assume that the secret to great returns is in picking the right stocks.

In many ways, this shift in focus is admirable, since it is at least a movement in the right direction. But the approach still comes from an overall failure to respect the problem and see the big picture for what it really is. An investor who knows better than to engage in market timing, and who avoids the management fees of mutual funds by doing his own stock picking is indeed ahead of the pack. But he is not yet the leader, and nor will he ever be unless he graduates to the next level of awareness.

For starters, many of the same problems with market timing exist with stock picking. The same rich matrix of layers still exists within each company, and across and within their competitors. The success or failure of a natural gas company, for instance, depends on the consuming behavior of literally hundreds of millions of people, the day-to-day conduct of employees, the decisions of management, and even the policy choices of federal, state, and local governments.

> "I think the biggest myth about the stock market is that there are expert investors who can consistently beat the market. It just isn't true."
> – Burton G. Malkiel, Professor of Economics
> *A Random Walk Down Wall Street*

Just read the memoirs and biographies of business leaders to see how often make-or-break decisions come down to a chance encounter or the mental state of the decision maker. You could even argue that Lehman Brother's would not have failed so completely if it hadn't been for CEO Dick Fuld's perpetual state of denial. As the end approached, even his subordinates shut him out of the negotiations with the few companies that could inject enough capital to save the firm. They knew that if Dick entered the room his state of denial would trigger a defensive reaction and he would chase any of the would-be saviors out of the room.

The major point here is, again, that we need to respect the problem. A company is a complex organism, with its own unique anatomy, gut bacteria, and the like. No two companies are the same, and no two CEOs are the same. On top of this, they are immersed in an incredibly diverse and complex economic ecosystem. You might pick the strongest and healthiest water buffalo but fail to see the crocodile three feet away.

> "Rip Van Winkle [is the] style of investing that we favor. Our stay-put behavior reflects our view that the stock market serves as a relocation center at which money is moved from the active to the patient. The much-maligned idle rich have received a bad rap: They have maintained or increased their wealth while many of the energetic rich have seen their fortunes disappear."
>
> – Warren Buffett

And here, just as we saw with market timing, the data shows us exactly what we'd expect to see given the incredible challenges of stock picking. More than two hundred studies have been published that compare the performance of stock-picking investment managers (primarily mutual fund managers) to the market as a whole, and of course, unsurprisingly, the results of these studies show that the vast majority of stock-picking managers underperform the market. According to one such study, the chances of a manager beating the market over a ten-year period were found to be 1-in-36.

Investing in an individual stock exposes the investor to two risks that are significantly minimized by buying broad indexes:

- Company risk
- Sector risk

John C. Bogle, founder of the Vanguard mutual fund family and a strong proponent of low-cost index investment strategies, conducted his own study, *Bogle on Equity Fund Selection*, in which he found similar results: Only 9 of the 355 actively managed mutual funds he reviewed beat the market over a thirty-year time frame. That's roughly 2.5% or 1-in-39 odds for picking a winning fund. Quite similar to the results of the more academic studies, and coincidentally, close to the odds of a roulette wheel.

Survivin' Ain't Thrivin'

GE, IBM, and Gillette are great examples to illustrate why it's not enough to merely pick the companies most likely to endure through the ages. GE suffered fifteen years of zero price appreciation from 1965 to 1980, and was later hit especially hard by the bear market of 2008. IBM and Gillette—both excellent companies—saw their stock prices fall by 65% during the 1960s and 1970s. Despite being among the few surviving companies on the original S&P 500® Index, these extended periods of decline and stagnation kept these companies from keeping up with the market as a whole. For much of that time, the market was evolving, adapting, and moving forward, while these companies were scraping along with their dinosaur bellies dragging in the dirt.

Chasing Performance

Many investors try to pick mutual funds and stocks that will outperform the market by simply chasing after last year's winners. Sadly, research by Lipper, a mutual fund rating service, has shown how this seemingly no-brainer strategy hurts more than it helps. By following a strategy that selects funds based on good, multi-year, *historical* results, investors managed to earn an annual return of just 3.7%—a far cry from the long-term 10% compounded return for indexes.

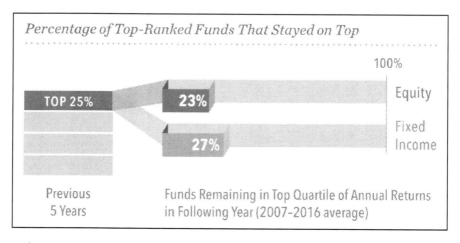

Figure 2-1: More often than not, the top performers in a given year end up underperforming in following years. Source: Dimensional Fund Advisors.

In hindsight, the results are not surprising: By following this strategy, investors were increasing the odds that they would be buying into a fund at a peak point in its performance. Later, when these funds would inevitably fall back down to a low point (i.e. revert to their mean or average performance), the investors would ditch the funds and reinvest their money in the next batch of funds with recently good returns, starting this wealth-destroying cycle over again.

"The rear-view mirror is one thing; the windshield is another."

– Warren Buffett

It's not too difficult to see how you'd get the same result by following this strategy for stock-picking. We'd see the same pattern of tending to pick a stock when it's at a momentary peak, and then devastated by our greater losses, selling in frustration at the bottom. It's likely, too, that the crushing loss itself only further motivates such investors to "swing for the fences" and do it again, like some kind of self-imposed manic-depressive episode. And of course, there are still the higher transaction costs and tax rates, that further compound the bad outcomes.

Mean Reversion

"Mean reversion" or "reversion to the mean" is a common phenomenon and topic of discussion in investing, finance, and economics. It refers to the tendency of many different types of measurements (investment returns, GDP, etc.) to converge back to their historical average value over time. Consequently, when a measure is way outside its norm, such as when a mutual fund has stellar performance in a given year, informed investors often expect those same measures to reverse over time in order to bring them back in line with their historical averages.

As a result, investors who chase performance by buying into hot stocks or funds end up suffering in two ways: The first is the reversion to the mean of the actual stock or fund, and the second is the reversion to the mean of the broader market (which is why we call such downward movements "corrections").

Predictions and Prognostications

Given the difficulty of timing the market or picking the right stocks, would access to the right combination of newspapers, magazines, books, and experts provide enough of an edge to overcome those extra transaction costs and taxes, and maybe even make enough profit to outperform the market?

The unfortunate reality is that newspapers, magazines, books, and experts often fare even worse than the investment newsletters we exposed in the sidebar ("The Folly of Trusting Newsletters") on page 24.

"We've long felt that the only value of stock forecasters is to make fortune tellers look good."

– Warren Buffett

"If there are 10,000 people looking at the stocks and trying to pick winners, well, one in 10,000 is going to score, by chance alone, a great coup, and that's all that's going on. It's a game. It's a chance operation, and people think they are doing something purposeful . . . but they're really not."

— Merton Miller, Nobel Laureate
The Trillion Dollar Bet

Newspapers and Magazines

In an article published in the *Financial Analysts Journal* ("Are Cover Stories Effective Contrarian Indicators?") three finance professors from the University of Richmond showed how an investor who relied on the favorable or unfavorable treatment of companies featured in magazine cover stories (i.e. their most in-depth article) would have done quite poorly. After being featured in a cover story (in *BusinessWeek, Fortune,* or *Forbes*), they found that the company would more often than not experience the exact opposite results of what one would expect—*favorable cover stories tended to be followed by periods of negative performance while unfavorable stories tended to be followed by periods of positive performance.* Individuals trading on such news, they concluded, were likely to fare poorly.

Of course, it shouldn't be too hard to see why this happens. It's a product of the subscription-based business model itself. Doom and gloom sells, and so do articles that scream over-the-top opportunity. Imagine a magazine that gave you the same good honest advice in each issue: "Buy quality companies using broad-based indexes, hold, periodically rebalance and sit tight through the corrections." *The publication would be out of business in a short time.* (For an entertaining parody of the kind of investment analysis that *does* get published in newspapers and magazines, see "The First Totally Honest Stock Market Story" on page 239.)

Jason Zweig: Sound Advice vs. What Sells

Jason Zweig, writer of "The Intelligent Investor" column for the *Wall Street Journal*, has been writing for years in support of the same basic approach. Like Warren Buffett, he praises low-cost index funds and encourages investors to avoid fads and emotional extremes—but the fact that this kind of repeated, sound advice does not sell led him to make some interesting comments:

> "My job is to write the exact same thing between 50 and 100 times a year in such a way that neither my editors nor my readers will ever think I am repeating myself."

> "It's no wonder that . . . people who receive frequent news updates on their investments earn lower returns than those who get no news. It's also no wonder that the media has ignored those findings. Not many people care to admit that they spend their careers being part of the problem instead of trying to be part of the solution."

> "Investing should be like watching paint dry or watching grass grow. If you want excitement, take $800 and go to Las Vegas."
>
> – Paul Samuelson, Economist
> Nobel Laureate

Figure 2-2. The prize for the most-wrong-ever cover story goes to *BusinessWeek* for proclaiming "The Death of Equities" in its August 13, 1979 issue. Three years later a bull market took off that lasted for eighteen years and was one of the longest and most significant in U.S. history.

Books

Flipping Houses for Dummies was published at the height of the real estate bubble in late 2006. This book promised to teach its readers how to "lay the foundation for successful flipping and bring home the bucks." Of course, by the time the book hit bookstores shelves, the housing market had already peaked and began to decline precipitously.

Figure 2-3: The real "dummies" in 2006 were those who heeded this advice.

Experts

At the end of 2007, *BusinessWeek* published its annual Summary of Economic Forecasts for 2008, based on a survey of fifty-four economists. All fifty-four economists predicted that the U.S. economy *would not* "sink into a recession." Instead they all declared that 2008 would be a solid though unspectacular year. We now know how spectacularly wrong they were.

Philip Tetlock, an American psychologist and political scientist, became so frustrated with the arrogance of punditry that he devised an unusual experiment. In 1984, Tetlock selected 284 academics, economists, and think-tank policy experts who were all considered experts and who made their livings predicting political and economic trends. He asked this group for their predictions about how the future might turn out. Twenty years later, he revisited their predictions and the results were astounding. Most of the experts, Tetlock showed, were no better at making predictions than "dart-throwing chimpanzees." Worse yet, when challenged about their mistakes, many of them failed to own up—some tried to fudge, while others claimed to have been right all along.

> "There are two kinds of forecasters: Those who don't know and those who don't know that they don't know."
>
> – John Kenneth Galbraith, Economist

Part of the problem lies in the lack of accountability within the profession of punditry itself. Make a bold prediction and the journalists and TV cameras come running; no one remembers when the prediction fails to materialize. Paul Ehrlich's 1968 book, *Population Bomb*, for example, argued that the earth's population was growing far more quickly than our ability to feed it. He painted a terrifying picture of mass starvation to come in the following decade. Instead, not only did his apocalypse fail to materialize, but the agricultural "green revolution" of the 1960s and 1970s actually led to a massive *decrease* in global starvation rates.

This kind of blundering error and the thinking behind it was wonderfully captured in a letter written in July 2009 by a group of eminent British economists and constitutional experts to the Queen of England, in which they attributed their failure to predict the credit crunch to "a failure of the collective imagination." Is that all we really get when we turn to the experts? The best that their "collective imaginations" have to offer? Apparently so, and it doesn't seem to be much good to begin with.

Rear View Driving

What newspapers, magazines, books, and experts all seem to have common is that they succumb to the same ailment that afflicts performance chasing mutual fund- and stock-pickers. They speed on down the highway while looking only in the rear-view mirror. And, in the end, we find that, in turning to outside sources in hopes of overcoming our own shortcomings, these outside sources are no less human than we are. And, worse, their business models, arrogance, and other factors often make them an even greater threat to our ability to make sound investment decisions.

> "Skepticism about past returns is crucial. The truth is, much as you may wish you could know which funds will be hot, you can't—and neither can the legions of advisors and publications that claim they can."
>
> – Bethany McLean, Author
> "The Skeptic's Guide to Mutual Funds"

For your own sake, for the sake of your financial, mental, and physical health—and for the sake of those you love—steer clear of stock-pickers, market-timers, and ignore the newspapers, magazines, and the dubious "experts" of the moment. Don't play their game, on their turf, by their rules.

> "There are two times when a man shouldn't speculate: when he can't afford it, and when he can."
>
> –Mark Twain

Chapter 3

Financial Advisors (and Mutual Funds)

> "The stockbroker services his clients the same way that Bonnie and Clyde serviced banks."
>
> – William J. Bernstein, Financial Theorist and Author
> *The Intelligent Asset Allocator*

It's hard to separate the problems with financial advisors from the problems with active mutual funds. They have an evolved symbiotic relationship, where the financial advisors need the fees they get from the mutual funds for peddling their products, and the mutual funds need an army of financial advisors to sell their less-than-desirable wares. As a result, while this chapter will focus mostly on financial advisors, there will be much to say that overlaps with problems with mutual funds as well.

The core problem is that financial advisors often don't tell their clients about the problems with mutual funds. Consequently, any critique of mutual funds becomes almost automatically a critique of financial advisors because it's just one more thing they aren't telling you so that they can keep on collecting their commissions and kick-backs from the mutual funds.

Ten Things Your Advisor Won't Tell You

Like most people, you probably look for the best in others. As such, you probably take your investment advisor at face value. Surely, he is a fine and ethical fellow, guided by a finely-tuned inner moral compass. You may even golf together and attend the same social functions. But no amount of shared laughs, experiences, and pats on the back can overcome the fact that his business puts his own interests directly at odds with your own.

> "Wall Street is the only place where people ride to work in a Rolls Royce to get advice from those who take the subway."
>
> – Warren Buffett

He puts bread on his table, for himself and his family, by generating as much revenue in fees for his business as possible. Every dollar he makes is one less dollar you get to keep. His greatest reward comes when he sells you the *wrong* mutual fund, because not only will he get the fees for that sale, but he will be able to get more fees later once the mutual fund loses money and he can convince you to switch into a different one. The last thing he wants (and the last thing most would ever recommend) would be for you to buy a low-cost index fund and hold it for five or ten years. *That would stop his flow of commissions!* Here are ten things your advisor probably forgot to tell you so that he could keep you on this fee-generating treadmill.

 Not all investment service companies are held to the same standards.

Financial firms and stockbrokers are often given incentives that encourage them to act against their customers' or clients' best interests. This shouldn't be too surprising when you think about it. If a company that makes investment products, such as mutual funds, is having a tough time selling some of its products, then it makes sense that they will try to motivate brokers to sell these products by offering better commissions. But if part of the reason they are having a tough time selling these investment products is that the products have not been performing well, then they are, in effect, paying commissions that encourage brokers to sell an inferior product.

Because this dynamic exists, and because regulators are aware of it, virtually all brokers, financial planners, and investment advisors are held to at least some kind of legal standard designed to protect their customers and clients. *The important thing to remember, for our purposes, is that different types of investment service providers are not necessarily held to the same standards when it comes to protecting their customers/clients.*

The typical brokerage firm, for instance, is generally <u>not</u> subject to a fiduciary duty—one of the highest levels of protection—while Registered Investment Advisors (RIAs) are.*

---

* This distinction between stockbrokers and RIAs is true as a matter of federal securities (investment) law. However, some courts, in specific

RIAs owe their clients a duty of undivided loyalty and utmost good faith. This means they are prohibited from engaging in any activity that conflicts with the interests of their clients and are required to proactively take steps reasonably necessary to fulfill these obligations. Stockbrokers, on the other hand, are only required to make a "suitability determination" when they provide investment advice or sell investment products. This means they have to make sure that what they advise and what they sell is "suitable" (but not necessarily optimal) for their customers/clients. When choosing between multiple "suitable" options, they can direct their customers/clients towards the ones that will compensate them the most, even if these are not the best choices from among the various "suitable" investment options.

> "Our investigation found a financial snake pit rife with greed, conflicts of interest, and wrongdoing."
>
> – *Wall St. and the Financial Crisis*
> US Senate Report, April 2011

Taking these two factors (incentives and standards) into consideration, in our view, the best approach is to do two things: First, look into the specific incentives (i.e. compensation structures) of the firm you are thinking about using for your investment needs to see if they are aligned with your own interests. This way you increase the chance that they actually will act in your best interest on an ongoing basis, without needing the threat of lawsuits to keep them straight. This is analogous to the carrot in the carrot-and-stick metaphor of motivation. The second thing is to use an investment

---

jurisdictions, have found that brokers do have a fiduciary duty under certain, limited circumstances.

services provider that is subject to the highest standards and duties (i.e. one that faces the greatest "stick" if they go astray). In practice, this means if anything were to happen and you actually did need to file a lawsuit, you would be setting yourself up to have an easier case to make.

Taken as a whole, therefore, we hold the view that it is best to use an RIA *and* to look at the internal compensation structure of that RIA before settling on which one you will use. In our view, you want an RIA who is compensated in a way (or who earns commissions in a way) that makes it so that their compensation increases proportionally if your funds grow and decreases proportionally if your funds shrink. Many of the investment services companies that will solicit you (or that you may seek out) will likely fall short of meeting these two criteria, so be aware of these distinctions and be sure to use them to your advantage in the selection process.

 Relatively little training is required to become an investment ~~salesman~~ advisor.

The skills and training required to become an investment advisor pale in comparison to those required of doctors, lawyers, and many other professions. To serve the public, all you have to do is pass an exam to sell life insurance and pass a few more on the securities industry.

After passing the exams and being approved by federal and the state regulators, new associates at a firm are likely to receive at least some additional training; however, this "training" is almost always focused on *sales training*. Few firms offer real training on investments or financial planning.

> "I had never managed money. I had never made any real money . . . yet I was holding myself out as a great expert on matters of finance. I was telling people what to do with millions of dollars when the largest financial complication I had ever encountered was a $325 overdraft in my account at the Chase Manhattan Bank."
>
> – Michael Lewis, Author
> *Liar's Poker*

The newly minted investment salesman (ahem...advisor) is usually given a sales manual and a commission sheet. He frequently tries to sell you investment or insurance products without fully appreciating the tax implications for your particular situation, the impact on your retirement income, or any potential estate-planning ramifications. Instead of understanding your specific financial requirements and circumstances, he offers a "canned" sales pitch that you could just as easily hear on a used car lot. He will be told to contact everyone he knows personally (family, friends, etc.) because this is his "warm market," before moving on to "cold call" strangers. This is your financial "advisor."

> "It is difficult to systematically beat the market. But it is not difficult to systematically throw money down a rat hole by generating commissions (and other costs). Investment managers sell for the price of a Picasso what routinely turns out to be paint-by-number art."
>
> – Patricia C. Dunn, former Vice Chairman
> Barclays Global Investors

HauK! HauK!

© 2017 www.RVWWealth.com

THAT IS HOWEY, OUR FORMER INVESTMENT ADVISOR. HE WENT ALONG WITH A CAREER CHANGE SUGGESTED BY HIS CLIENTS.

You might think you know about the hidden costs, but there are more than you realize.

Buying or selling a stock almost always requires paying a commission of some kind to the broker. In a similar way, mutual fund shares are often sold with a sales charge known as a "load." These are the charges that are easy to spot. But there are also less obvious fees and downright hidden fees that are easy to miss.

The annual fees paid to mutual fund managers and the costs of all their trades typically don't show up anywhere in the information they share other than in the fine print. Then there are the costs associated with the tax inefficiency of mutual funds, which are even harder to see, since you won't get any of the numbers until the end of the year, and even then, most investors simply send their K-1's and 1099 tax forms to their tax preparer totally unaware of the tax costs generated by their portfolio.

All these different layers of expenses are eventually disclosed in some obscure way or another, but rarely are they ever explained in a clear and intelligible way in the prospectuses that investment advisors hand out to their clients. Yet these expenses can add up to as much as 25% of the total returns, effectively cannibalizing that part of your returns over time. What could have been a 10% annual return is reduced to just 7.5%.

> Optimal portfolios comprise liquid, transparent investments where costs are minimized and where the investor understands the role of every element.

The costs and fees are not limited to mutual funds either. Many investors are sold the idea to invest in equities through "tax-deferred" variable annuity products. Agents earn high commissions on these products, and there are extra layers of internal expenses that can be very costly. Even worse, there are additional fees ("surrender charges") for those who decide to liquidate these annuities prematurely.

 In addition to hidden costs, there are also indirect costs you should know about.

When an investment advisor recommends a fund to a client, most of the time the fund will be a load fund of the kind we mentioned earlier. The broker gets to collect a portion of the load fee as a reward for getting you to choose one fund over another. This fee is a *direct* cost. But there are also *indirect* costs your investment advisor should be telling you about—the biggest of which is that load funds frequently underperform no-load funds *even after removing the negative effects of the fees*.

The Load Road is the Slow Road

Morningstar, Inc., a leading provider of independent investment research, conducted a recent study and found that even when the negative effects of the loads are excluded from fund performance, no-load funds still did better than load funds.

In other words, when you buy into a load fund, you are not paying more for outperformance, *you're often paying more for underperformance*. This makes sense when you think about it from the perspective of a mutual fund manager. If your performance alone isn't good enough to attract more investors, you need to find a way to pay more salesmen to promote the product, which means you have to charge more fees to pay for all the sales and marketing. Funds that don't impose load fees, on the other hand, have repeatedly outperformed those that do and so can spend less on sales and marketing.

 You pay for the gun that shoots you.

If a man asked you to buy him a gun so that he could shoot you, you'd rightly be appalled. And if a salesman asked you to pay him some money so that he could go do some research on how to find more ways to get between you and your money, again, you'd rightly be appalled. Yet everyday people do just that when they send more and more money to mutual funds and active managers.

Believe it or not, mutual fund companies have the audacity to compute the return on their funds net of their *marketing* expenses. In other words, they skim some of the gains off the top to fund their own advertising efforts. These expenses include the costs of advertising and selling fund shares, compensating brokers and investment advisors, and printing and mailing sales literature.

So, while you lay there, suffering from the below-market, after-fee returns of a mutual fund, those very same fees are being used to convince your neighbor and everyone else that this very same mutual fund is the most amazing thing ever. And since your neighbor's and everyone else's mutual funds are all doing the same thing, we find ourselves caught up in this strange cycle of mutually-funded mutual fund destruction.

> Most of the major fund families have lists of funds. Each year they pick the best few to advertise, many of which end up performing poorly the following year. It's a rotating shill game of picking previous winners. The evidence shows clearly that the best performers tend to subsequently underperform because of reversion to the mean and the rotation of cycles within the market.

If that's not bad enough, even for a talented and well-meaning mutual fund manager, it becomes harder and harder to profitably run a larger and larger mutual fund. As the marketing efforts draw more money into the fund, the fund's performance will likely suffer. Consequently, the marketing efforts you're paying for can actually become a *cause* of lower performance, in addition to the hit you're already taking directly for paying the fees out of your returns.

Certain investments or insurance products pay the advisor more than other investments.

Mutual fund families often employ a special type of sales staff known as "internal wholesalers" to promote their funds to the front-line salesmen (ahem, advisors). As many companies know, one of the best ways to boost sales is to boost commissions or offer greater incentives to the sales force. This ultimately leads to a higher priced product, an inferior product, or both. As a result, in the investment business, the best products for the client end up getting the least promotion. Since these funds keep their costs low by avoiding the whole back-scratching game and paying little or no commissions to the middlemen, there are few incentives for those middlemen, brokers, and other intermediaries to promote them.

> You *thought* you heard the advisor say, "If you don't make money, I don't make money," but what he really meant was, "If you don't make money, I still make money . . . just not as much."

 Mutual fund shares are sold in "classes" — A, B, and C—and all three are bad for you.

The various fee structures of mutual funds confuse investors, and whether this is intentional or not, this makes it easier for investment advisors and fund managers to make more money.

Class A shares charge a front-end "load," reducing the

amount of your money that makes it into the fund. A 5% load means that only $9,500 of every $10,000 invested goes to work for you. Class A fund shares are typically charged a 12b-1 fee, limited to a maximum of 0.25%. "Breakpoints," which are simply volume discounts, reduce the amount of the up-front sales load. The first breakpoint for many load funds usually occurs when an account holder has at least $50,000 invested in the fund. Loads continue to drop at various breakpoints (such as $100,000, $250,000, and $500,000) until they disappear entirely, typically at $1,000,000.

> "You know the stories: 'The Top Ten Mutual Funds to Buy Now,' 'How to Double Your Money This Year,' personality profiles that read like fan magazines. Stock touting pieces that praise any path to profits. We've all done these stories, in one form or another. It's investment pornography."
>
> – Jane Bryant Quinn, Financial Writer
> *Newsweek* Contributor

Class B shares don't charge a front-end load, but charge a higher 12b-1 management fee instead, typically the maximum 0.75%. On top of this, the shares frequently carry a "back-end load," called a *contingent deferred sales charge* (CDSC). Investors have to pay this fee if they sell their shares within a few years of purchase. Mutual fund companies and investment advisors claim that the deferred sales charge encourages long-term holding by imposing a penalty for selling too early. But in this case, "selling too early" means within five to seven years of purchasing the shares. A year or two after this "too soon" period passes, the Class B shares are converted to Class A shares, and the 12b-1 fee is reduced. Class B shares are often misrepresented as "no-load" mutual fund shares, when what they really are is back-loaded instead of front-loaded.

Class C shares typically charge the maximum permissible 12b-1 fee, a total of 1%, and carry a small CDSC of 1% to 2% for the first year after you buy the shares. Class C shares do not convert to Class A shares, and the 12b-1 fee remains high the entire time you own the fund.

All of this is confusing to most investors, and this is how some investment advisors profit. When they sell Class A shares, they receive the front-end load. When they sell Class B shares, the distributor uses its own money to pay a commission. Because investment advisors can make more money by selling Class B shares to large clients (even when it's not in the client's interest), mutual funds (in response to pressure from regulators) no longer permit the purchase of Class B shares when the amount invested would qualify for breakpoints. Failing to advise a client of an available breakpoint is now considered a sales violation.

 Wrap accounts are just a way to pile fees upon fees in a single account.

A popular investment account sold by investment advisors is known as a "wrap account." This is an account where all account expenses are bundled into a single (flat or fixed) fee. Charges of 1%–2% of the account's assets are deducted from the balance at regular intervals to pay for all trading, administrative, research, and advisory expenses. And there are usually several other layers of undisclosed fees that affect the account.

Investment advisors sell these accounts under the claim that they protect investors from over-trading or "churning," which under a different type of account might be done by the advisor to generate more commissions. In a wrap account, the advisor does not receive a commission. Excessive trading in a customer's account to generate extra commissions can happen, so the theory is not without merit. Because the wrap account is charged a flat annual fee, the most you can be charged—at least on the surface—is the fixed percentage.

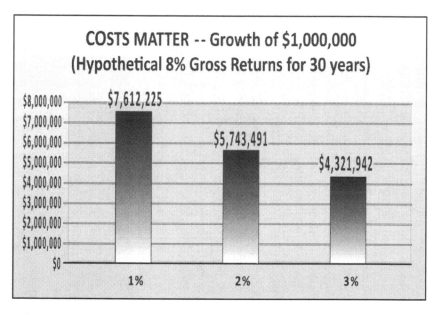

Figure 3-1: The negative effects of mutual fund sales fees, annual investment expenses, and advisory "wrap" fees should not be ignored. The difference between a 1% fee and a 3% fee is substantial in the long run.

But when wrap accounts hold mutual funds or funds of funds, which is often the case, you might actually be charged twice. The fund manager charges his fee inside each fund, and that internal expense shows up as lower annual returns. Half of the stock market's average gains could be lost to the combination of a fund's internal expenses and the external investment advisor's annual fee.

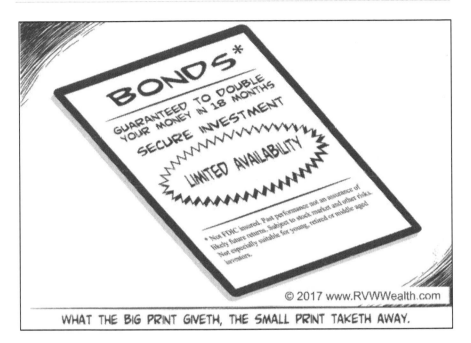

WHAT THE BIG PRINT GIVETH, THE SMALL PRINT TAKETH AWAY.

Eventually, the SEC realized that wrap accounts do not help investors and took action to stop this industry abuse. In late 2007, they ordered brokers and advisors to stop offering wrap accounts. The industry responded with prompt compliance, and converted many client wrap accounts into another type of account known as a *fee-based, nondiscretionary advisory account*. In these accounts, investment advisors can offer comprehensive advice, but the investor controls the final decisions. But since the fees are still assessed as a percentage of assets in the account and the account can still hold fee-bearing mutual funds, the layering of fees is still in place and not much has really changed.

These accounts provide an opportunity for the investment advisor to portray the costs more attractively, positioning himself, the salesman, as an "objective" judge of value. By effectively moving to the other side of the table, alongside the investor, the "Investment Advisor" secures a large regular income and positions himself to retain you and, more importantly, your assets, even if a particular fund he recommends performs poorly.

There is no evidence to suggest that "house funds" are good investments.

Many of the major Wall Street brokerage firms run their own "house funds," which they argue will be a good investment because these Wall Street powerhouses have access to the best information and analysis on which to base their investment decisions for the fund. If this were actually true, however, you would expect their funds to be among the top performers year after year. Instead, studies have shown that no such evidence exists. In fact, many of these house funds actually do worse than independent actively managed mutual funds—which aren't that great to begin with.

Then why do brokers try to get their clients to buy into these funds? The answer is simple: House funds typically pay higher commissions and offer other incentives. To many in the investment advice business, the most important part of the job is making sales. There are a few (a tiny minority) who work only for hourly compensation, but the vast majority of stockbrokers are paid based on their sales. One way to do this is by encouraging hyperactive trading, which boosts the *quantity* of commissions they collect. But if they are dealing with a client uninterested in constant trading, they can make up for this by increasing the *size* of the commissions they get for each trade. House funds are a great way for them to do this.

Most brokers require you to submit to binding arbitration.

In almost all cases, investors agree that they will submit to binding arbitration in the event of a dispute with their broker. This generally goes hand-in-hand with opening a brokerage account and can be found in the fine print of whatever documents were signed. These brokers will argue that this is for your benefit, so that you won't have to actually go to court to settle your disputes. The arbitration, in this case, goes through a system run by the Financial Industry Regulatory Authority (FINRA).

While it might sound reassuring to have your disputes go through a system setup by FINRA ("Surly a regulatory authority will look out for the little guy!") FINRA is actually a private corporation (what's called a "self-regulatory organization" or SRO), and the arbitration system itself is setup in a way that tends to favor repeat players, i.e. financial firms that have a continuous stream of cases going before the arbitrators.

The two parties in a dispute select a panel of three arbitrators similar to how two opposing attorneys might select a jury for a court trial. Each party has the power to veto a certain number of arbitrators from the list they are given by FINRA. They then rank the ones that are left. FINRA then compares the ranked lists from both parties and picks a panel that takes the preferences of both parties into account. The problem here is that the arbitrators are often professional arbitrators who depend on being selected repeatedly for cases for a significant part of their income. When a major brokerage firm has case after case brought before the arbitrators, this creates an incentive for the arbitrators to not upset the brokerage firms so that they will be more likely to be selected again for the next case. Since most investors are not repeat players, this has led some to suspect that there is an overall bias within the system that favors financial firms over individual investors.

> "There are two kinds of investors, be they large or small: those who don't know where the market is headed and those who don't know what they don't know. Then again, there is a third type of investor: the investment professional, who indeed knows he doesn't know, but whose livelihood depends upon appearing to know."
>
> – William J. Bernstein, Financial Theorist and Author
> *The Intelligent Asset Allocator*

A study conducted by securities lawyer Daniel Solin and Edward O'Neal, a former finance professor, shows that the arbitration win rate, meaning the percentage of cases where investors win "damages" from brokers, was only 44% in 2004. Recent studies show that the win rate has varied little since that time: 47% in 2009, 45% in 2010, and 44% in 2011. And the win rate tells us nothing about whether or not the "damages" awarded were enough to cover the actual harm done. To get access to that kind of information, the researchers actually had to sue the organization. Based on the 14,000 arbitration records they were able to obtain, they found that the larger the claim, the smaller the success rate. *For those with claims over $250,000, only 12% were successful.* And, as it turns out, each year mutual funds were either first or second on the list in terms of the number of complaints where mutual funds were the underlying product involved.

What Does It All Mean?

What conclusions can we draw from this laundry list of problems and issues with financial advisors, funds, and their unholy alliance? If you are among the great multitude of investors whose advisors peddle actively managed mutual funds, wrap accounts, and the like, without even a mention of the points above, then you might want to reconsider whose side your "advisor" is really on.

Chapter 4

Hedge Funds

> "Buy low-cost index funds, which will outperform the majority of other investors—the vast majority—and **avoid hedge funds.**"
> – Warren Buffett

Anyone who reads *The Wall Street Journal* knows the popularity and infamy of hedge funds. These ubiquitous, yet obscure, investment vehicles are known for producing heaven-bound investment returns on the one hand and earth-shattering blow-ups on the other. But what is a hedge fund, after all? Given their popularity, you'd think more people would know what the phrase actually means.

The first word, "hedge", refers to the way these types of funds historically focused on reducing risk by hedging against broader market movements. They would "short" the market and go "long" the stocks they thought would do well. When the market would crash, they would (in theory) be unaffected because of how the losses on their long positions would be offset by the gains on their short positions. Conversely, if the market jumped and lifted all stocks, they would also be unaffected—giving up general market gains as well as general market losses. But if one of their stocks did well because of its own unique circumstances (which is what they were betting on), the gains would not be cancelled out with the broader market and the fund itself would profit.

The First Hedge Fund

In 1945, Alfred W. Jones, a financial journalist, launched what would come to be known as the first hedge fund. Jones bought stocks he thought were undervalued and then he "hedged" his bets by selling short the stocks he thought were over-valued. While this strategy, known as *long/short*, is still in use by many hedge funds today, the term "hedge fund" has come to refer more to a particular structure of investment rather than a particular strategy.

To execute this strategy, the funds needed to be able to take large short positions, which was prohibited for funds that fell under the securities regulations from the 1930s. Consequently, these funds had to carefully organize their legal structures and limit the types of investors who could invest with them to avoid triggering the provisions in the 1930s regulations. If they set off any of these triggers, they would become subject to the associated rules and limitations that other types of funds (such as mutual funds) have to follow.

Over time, the term "hedge fund" came to refer less to funds that follow the original hedging investment strategy and more to any fund that was so structured to avoid triggering the 1930s regulations. This is the dominant meaning of "hedge fund" as the phrase is used today. In other words, what's called a "hedge fund" today is essentially a fund that is legally structured a certain way and that limits the types of investors it accepts so as to minimize the amount of regulatory oversight and restrictions and thereby maximize the fund's flexibility to engage in more exotic and more highly-levered trades than would otherwise be allowed. This is why hedge funds are infamous for their lack of transparency and why there is such a wide variety of "hedge funds" today.

Hedge funds today employ numerous strategies, including capital arbitrage, distressed debt, event-driven, multi-strategy, and many more. To be fair, the majority of hedge funds do still make some attempt (whether through complex algorithms or old-fashioned hedging) to produce low-risk returns or returns that are uncorrelated with the general stock market. But since there is no universal agreement on how best to do this and there are still no guarantees that this is even what a "hedge fund" will be trying to do, we cannot assume there is any hedging involved just because a fund is called a "hedge fund" by itself or others.

Consumer Protection

The 1930s securities regulations were essentially consumer protection laws. They were designed to prevent "unsophisticated" investors from getting involved with investment strategies that were either too risky or too complex for their level of sophistication. Increased transparency was another purpose behind these regulations, since no investor—no matter how sophisticated—can make wise investment decisions when he or she isn't told the whole story.

What makes one investor "sophisticated" and another "unsophisticated"? Unfortunately, since the regulators aren't in a position to make all investors take an examination, they have generally decided to use various measures of net worth and/or income to decide whether or not an investor is "sophisticated" enough to invest in hedge funds. The logic is that, even if a very wealthy person is not sophisticated, they at least have the financial resources to hire attorneys and other more sophisticated people to look out for their interests. Given the points we just made about investment advisors in the last chapter, it seems like this assumption might be a bit of a stretch. Since when has *having money* been a safeguard against being swindled? More often, it seems to make you a target.

The Fatal Flaws of Hedge Fund Investing

Broadly speaking, there are two major flaws that make hedge funds poor investments—both of which fly under the radar of most investors and make hedge funds look more like a lucrative opportunity than the traps they often turn out to be. The first of the two flaws results from the out-sized fees that hedge funds charge investors. Even when hedge funds produce above market returns, their investors are often left with below market returns once the fees are taken into account. The second flaw is a collection of unusual risks that hedge funds face that are unlike those of other investment vehicles. These risks are so unique and different that even seasoned hedge fund investors are often unaware of their existence.

Hedge funds are where greed, trust, and hope meet the roulette table.

Performance *After* Fees

For anybody with the perceived skill and the relationships necessary to open up a hedge fund, the rationale is obvious. Hedge fund managers often make the typical 2/20 ("two and twenty") fee structure, that gives them 2% of the assets under management plus an additional 20% of the profits. That means a manager with a $100 million fund will take home $2 million . . . *even if his fund lost money.* If, on the other hand, the fund is up 10% (which would be a $10 million profit), then he gets to pocket another $2 million (20% of the $10 million). By merely matching the 10% long-term average return of a stock market index, he takes home $4 million while his investors get their 10% return knocked down to a 6% net return after taking into account the fees.

Hedge funds also have most of the same turnover-related higher tax cost issues as mutual funds.

According to Hedgefund.net, by one measure of hedge fund returns (the HFN Aggregate index) hedge funds returned an average of 0.77% in 2016. Meanwhile, the total return for the S&P 500® Index was 11.96% and the total return for the Dow Jones Industrial Average was 16.5%. Longer term returns are generally similarly poor.

Lifting the Veil

Because of their lack of transparency and complexity, hedge funds are indeed inappropriate for most investors, and it is understandable why the 1930s regulations were designed to keep unsophisticated investors from participating in these funds. But even for those with an appetite for risk and the means and sophistication to play in this space, it is essential to tread carefully and to be well-armed with the facts before diving in. And further, because of the greater risks of fraud and other risks unique to hedge funds, it is even more important that this asset class be given only a small place, if any, in a well-designed portfolio.

The unique risks involved in hedge fund investing that either do not exist for non-hedge fund investments or are much, much higher with hedge funds, are: complexity risks, leverage, liquidity, relationship risks, and fraud.

"We have a higher percentage of the intelligentsia engaged in buying and selling pieces of paper. A great civilization will bear a lot of abuse, but there are dangers in the current situation that threaten anyone who swings for the fences."

– Charlie Munger,
Vice Chairman of Berkshire Hathaway

Leverage

People who become hedge fund managers do so because they think they know something that everyone else does not know, or that they understand something better, or that they can do something better. Either way, they all believe that they have an edge that sets them apart from the others. The edge they have, though, is often just a small one, and so the challenge is finding a way to take that small edge and make it into big results—big enough to grab investors' attention.

> "When you combine ignorance and leverage, you get some pretty interesting results."
>
> – Warren Buffett

The universally accepted way to do this is to use a large amount of leverage (i.e. debt) to maximize the returns. They purchase securities with borrowed money, resulting in both amplified gains and losses. But due to the opaque nature of these funds, its often hard for investors to tell just how much "juice" they are really using, making it, in turn, difficult to know exactly how much risk they are taking.

Liquidity

A commonly overlooked risk factor is that many hedge funds invest in relatively illiquid assets (meaning assets that are infrequently bought and sold), including derivatives and financial instruments that are difficult to understand. Because it is so difficult for the manager to quickly exit from these positions, they need to make it equally hard for their own investors to pull their money out of the fund. For this reason, withdrawals from hedge funds are usually only allowed a few times a year, and rarely more often than once per quarter. Sometimes hedge fund managers can even unilaterally modify the terms of the investment contract, imposing stiff penalties for withdrawal or even enacting emergency provisions that freeze investors funds so that they cannot withdraw for as long as the alleged "emergency" is in place.

Another problem that results from hedge funds' tendency

to trade in illiquid securities is that astute traders at rival hedge funds can develop strategies designed to take advantage of the inherent weaknesses that come from holding illiquid positions. Once these rival hedge funds find out about this vulnerability and get themselves into a position to exploit it, they can squeeze the target hedge fund for all it's worth. This is part of why hedge funds are often so determined to maintain the utmost secrecy about their trading activities and fight any regulatory efforts that push for greater transparency. For investors, this lack of transparency — though it does protect the fund and its trades — creates an even greater risk that the hedge fund will stray from its original strategy. Typically, when funds do this, they move in the direction of taking even more bold, dangerous, and often desperate moves without telling their investors. In this way, illiquidity, and the resulting need for secrecy, set a stage ripe for dangerous dealings or even outright fraud (which we will cover shortly). This is also why the investors in a failing hedge fund are so often caught completely by surprise when their hedge fund suddenly implodes.

Complexity Risks

If the "edge" that a hedge fund has over other hedge funds is based on something simple and easy to copy, then that particular edge is not going to last for very long. As a result, the hedge fund industry tends to favor complex strategies and theories almost as ends in themselves. But the problem with complex strategies and theories is that their creators often succumb to the fatal flaw of thinking their complex methods provide a larger window into reality than they really do. They mistake complexity for comprehensiveness, when the two are not the same. This makes the fund more vulnerable to blind spots when they hit, since the fund will be even less prepared due to its false sense of certainty.

> "In many ways, a simpler approach to investing is more challenging than a complex approach because simple can be harder to adhere to. Simple doesn't make for a compelling sales pitch. It's not sexy. No one brags about simplifying their investment strategy to their peers. People assume simple means simplistic."
>
> – Ben Carlson, CFA, Director of Institutional Asset Management at Ritholtz Wealth Management

Even before an unforeseen crisis hits (something unpredicted by the models), the overconfidence and overreliance on the models tends to magnify the other risks already inherent in hedge fund investing: The managers will tend to take on more leverage than they otherwise would, thinking their models are airtight. They'll also tend to jump more eagerly into illiquid positions, thinking that if they're ever in a pinch and can't find someone willing to pay full price for their holdings, they can just show any potential buyers what these holdings are worth based on their theoretical models. This almost never works in practice. Relationship risks (which we'll cover next) are also made worse by overconfidence, especially when it comes from self-perceived genius (*"I am the one who conquered complexity!"*). This breeds an arrogance that creates resentment among rival and partner firms.

Relationship Risks

Related to liquidity and complexity risks are what we will call "relationship risks." This is an inescapable aspect of the fact that hedge funds have the freedom and desire to engage in the more *exotic* activities that they believe will give them the best risk reward tradeoffs.

Think of how different the roles are of a broker/dealer of baseball cards and a broker/dealer of endangered butterflies. There are countless forums and shops devoted to buying and selling baseball cards. If one were to cut you off or disappear altogether, it wouldn't matter—you could find plenty of other places to buy and sell baseball cards. But for the black-market trade in endangered butterflies, there are only a handful of shady characters willing to risk prison time to take part in this obscure but lucrative business. If just a few of these key players were to cut you out of the trade, you might suddenly find yourself completely out of the game.

Like it or not, this same dynamic exists in the realm of money management. The more complex, cutting-edge, or exotic the strategies are, the harder it is to find the right instruments for these trades and firms equally willing to trade in them. This is the essence of illiquidity—when few are interested in the product, there are few active buyers and sellers, which means it's hard to get deals done without buying at a large premium or selling at a deep discount. Investment banks play a key role in cultivating and maintaining these markets, trying to make them as liquid as they can. Consequently, it is vital for hedge funds trading in such instruments to have very healthy and close relationships with the investment banks that make markets for those instruments. And just like the trade in endangered butterflies, if the relationships sour and a hedge fund gets cut out, the hedge fund can suddenly find itself out of the game completely, forced to sell at deep discounts.

This is what happened to the hedge fund Long Term Capital Management (see sidebar "Long Term Capital Management" on page 68). Over time, they became arrogant and demanded offensive terms from their investment banks. This led to a growing resentment from both the investment banks and rival hedge funds. As a result, as soon as there was a crack in LTCM's armor, the other hedge funds were all too eager to exploit it and cause LTCM more pain. At the same time, none of the investment banks were eager to step in and help.

Buffett's Bet with Hedge Funds

In 2007, Warren Buffett issued a challenge to the hedge fund industry based on the idea that the performance of hedge funds could not justify their exorbitant fees. Protégé Partners accepted his challenge and the two placed a million-dollar bet, with Buffett taking the position that, including fees, costs and expenses, an S&P 500 index fund (the Vanguard Admiral Shares S&P 500 Index Fund) would outperform Protégé's hand-picked portfolio of hedge funds over the 10-year period ending December 31, 2017.

By the end of the first nine years, Buffett's index fund was up 85.4%, while Protégé's hand-picked basket of hedge funds was up only 22.0%. In Buffett's own words, there is "no doubt" about who will come out on top when the contest ends December 31, 2017.

Even the famed Michael Burry, featured in *The Big Short*, had to fight tooth and nail to hang on to his investment positions that were betting on the 2007/2008 housing and financial crisis. Even though he was spot-on with his prediction and trades, there was a very real risk that the souring relationships with his investors would force him to close out his trades before his predictions came true. Fortunately for him, and fortunately for—and in spite of—his investors, he was able to hang on long enough to produce for them an impressive profit. The real takeaway of this story, though, is not about the profits. It's the fact that, even if everything else goes right on a trade, there is still a very real risk that spiteful competitors, short-sighted partners, or other individuals outside of your control and the control of the hedge fund manager will get in the way and turn a huge profit into a wipe-out.

Long Term Capital Management

Perhaps the most famous hedge fund failure was that of Long Term Capital Management, or "LTCM," in late 1998. The fund was started in 1994 by an all-star team of Wall Street traders. At first, it seemed to deliver investors outstanding returns regardless of the market environment, and with very little risk (indeed, this was the plan, as predicted by their complex theories). The fund nearly tripled the value of its investors' assets from 1994 to the end of 1997.

But the fund's strategy involved looking for tiny variations that were often too small for other investors to notice, and too small to allow for much of a profit opportunity. Consequently, the fund had to constantly "lever up" (i.e. take on debt) for each trade to magnify the returns. Since the fund manager and the traders believed so fervently in their own complex theories, which said these trades were virtually risk-free, they rarely hesitated to take on as much debt as they needed to make their trades attractive.

In addition to the large amounts of debt they were taking on with each new trade, the fact that they were targeting such narrow and specific market anomalies meant they had to use more exotic and tailor-made derivative contracts, which can often only be gotten from the minority of investment banks willing to write these contracts and make a market for them. This made LTCM excessively dependent on a very small number of investment banks to both get in and get out of their trades (this is what we call "relationship risk"). The small market and throughput for trading also created many latent liquidity problems just waiting to pop.

In August 1998, LTCM (seemingly out of nowhere) suffered a one-month loss of 44%. In a remarkable case of understatement, fund manager John Meriwether said to his investors, "August has been very painful for all of us." Two months later, in October, the fund was insolvent (having lost more than $4.6 billion) and the Federal Reserve was forced to step in and stabilize markets.

Fraud

The Ponzi scheme run by Bernie Madoff for more than a decade was run under the cloaking guise of a hedge fund. But it is not quite accurate to say he was merely pretending to run a hedge fund as a cover for his mastermind Ponzi scheme. Nor is it true to say that if it had really been a "true" hedge fund there never would have been a problem or that he would have been caught sooner. More often than not, unfortunately, the truth is the exact opposite.

It is the lack of transparency with hedge funds and the high expected returns that *cause* often well-meaning hedge fund managers to slowly transform their failing hedge funds into Ponzi schemes. It all starts with their first year of poor performance. Unable or unwilling to admit their own failure and how they have failed their investors, they instead decide to fudge the numbers and tell their investors that they had a great year with phenomenal returns. Hearing the great news, new investors pour even more money into the fund. The fund manager, then, gladly accepts these funds, thinking, "If I can make a 30% return on this even bigger pile of money, I can report instead an acceptable 15% return and use the extra money to backfill last year's performance and make everything whole again!" The problem, of course, is that this wishful thinking almost never works out. Instead, the fund fails to meet the mark it needs to make things whole, and so they repeat the process again the next year, over and over until what was actually started as a legitimate hedge fund has fully transformed (thanks to the lack of transparency) into a full-blown Ponzi scheme.

Along the way, even when the hedge fund produces startling results (such as Madoff's 5-8% returns when the market was down 33-38% in 2008), investors and even investigators shrug it off, thinking, "After all, this is the kind of performance hedge funds are supposed to have." Other red flags are similarly ignored, overlooked, or explained away as some aspect of the complex algorithms being used or some quirk of the Midas touch of some fund manager elevated to the status of a modern-day oracle.

> Madoff's fraud was also facilitated by the fact that there was no distinction between two critical parties to asset management: The manager and the custodian/broker.

It is no coincidence, then, that these funds-gone-Ponzi are usually exposed and collapse during times of financial distress. Once the investors find themselves in need of more funds to tend to their own emergencies, they withdraw their funds from the one investment that hasn't gone down in value like everything else. But as more and more investors clamor to exit the now-hollow fund, the managers panic, and picking up on their wavering tone, so too do the inventors. Chaos ensues and where there was once the mirage of an unshakable edifice, there is nothing—no funds, no longer even the façade.

The Paradox: Why Do Hedge Funds Keep Growing?

If hedge funds are so problematic, why have they continued to grow so much as a segment of the investment industry? To answer this question, we need to first take a few steps back to understand why hedge funds are created and how they raise money.

In fact, for many managers, their very *raison d'être* is to raise as much capital as possible, since merely increasing total assets under management is often an easier way to generate fee income than attempting to beat the market and achieving actual capital appreciation for their investors.

> The words "risk-adjusted returns" are often a convenient way to hide poor performance behind a phrase and a computation that most investors do not understand and isn't relevant to them.

Consequently, hedge fund managers have just as much, or even more, of an incentive to grow the asset under management through marketing and promotional efforts than they do for growing the assets under management by generating superior returns. This has led to the creation of a sub-industry within the hedge fund industry that helps hedge fund managers raise more money. This sub-industry is filled with dot-connecting consultants, and their clients are the hedge fund managers. Since managing hedge funds is so lucrative, hedge fund managers can afford to pay these middlemen (something akin to hedge fund brokers) as much as 15%-25% of the manager's profits on whatever new funds are invested. Because this, too, is a lucrative profession, even more and more people have been drawn into the business of figuring out how to get more money into the hands of hedge funds.

Buffett Explains

In a 2016 letter to shareholders, Warren Buffett gave his own explanation for why hedge funds continue to grow despite their poor performance:

> "The wealthy are accustomed to feeling that it is their lot in life to get the best food, schooling, . . . you name it. Their money, they feel, should buy them something superior compared to what the masses receive. [These] financial 'elites'—wealthy individuals, pension funds, college endowments and the like—have great trouble meekly signing up for a financial product or service that is available as well to people investing only a few thousand dollars . . . [They] feel they deserve something 'extra' in investment advice. Those advisors who cleverly play to this expectation will get very rich."

If what Buffett says is true, then it is the combination of investor greed and Wall Street's salesmanship that keeps driving the growth of hedge funds, despite their generally poor performance.

In the end, this creates a paradox: Investors *should not* invest in hedge funds *because* of the high fees, yet investors *do* invest in hedge funds *because* of the high fees. The resolution to this paradox lies in seeing how the fees paid by the first group of investors come back around to finance the marketing campaigns to bring in the next round of investors.

> Hedge funds and 'alternatives' are Wall Street's equivalent of a phony Tiffany blue gift box—filled with hope and trust, and wrapped in small print.

There's another reason hedge funds keep growing, despite their aggressive fee structures, which is that many large institutions, such as pension funds and university endowments, are faced with requirements (deadlines, effectively) that say they need to put whatever money they have at their disposal profitably to work as soon as possible. Often, these large institutional investors are run by committees and boards whose members enjoy exchanging favors and rubbing elbows with whoever can or will make them feel more special than they already do.

They also sometimes do additional business with the managers or have special fee arrangements that provide better terms than other (smaller) investors. For all these reasons, Wall Street has a vested interest in continuing to bolster the hedge fund industry.

Fund of Funds

Investors are sometimes lured to an outgrowth of the hedge fund industry called a "fund of funds" (FOF). These investment vehicles are basically just hedge funds that invest in other hedge funds—it really is that simple. Consequently, there is another layer of fees that gets added on top of the already high fees that go to the underlying hedge funds. Why, then, would anyone want to invest in such a thing?

Here's the pitch: By investing in a FOF, you won't have to worry about picking the right hedge funds because the manager of the FOF will do all the necessary due diligence and pick the best hedge funds for you. Then, after making the initial investments in all these hedge funds, the manager of the FOF will keep an eye on the funds to make sure they are sticking with their stated strategies and that they aren't getting into anything riskier than what they said they'd be doing. This will help reduce the chances of there being a blow up or an incipient fraud at one of the hedge funds. If that's not enough, the FOF also provides diversification by being invested in multiple hedge funds. That way, if one hedge fund blows up, it won't take down the whole FOF with it. Lastly, FOFs, as larger players with larger pools of cash, can get access to the most popular and famous hedge funds by their greater bargaining power.

> "All the time and effort people devote to picking the right fund, the hot hand, or the great manager have, in most cases, led to no advantage."
>
> – Peter Lynch, American Investor
> and Mutual Fund Manager

That's the pitch. Here's the catch: As we've already seen, hedge funds themselves have many unique and unusual risks due to their own unique nature and the lack of transparency. So, taking a group of these economic creatures and then organizing them into a "pack" under the leadership of another creature of the same kind is like assigning an alpha male wolf to keep us safe from his own pack. The threats and dangers are not reduced but rather magnified. In 2008, huge groups of hedge funds got frozen out of the ability to trade and the price for their illiquidity became manifest.

The performance of these funds, then, depends on a multiplicity of managers, often each using different strategies and investment styles. Sometimes these funds will employ leverage, at the fund level, in an attempt to enhance returns, albeit with an additional measure of risk.

Di-*worse*-ification

Often investors who seek to diversify through funds of funds end up di-*worse*-ifying. Due to the lack of transparency, it's often hard to say whether a fund of funds is really adding uncorrelated investments (the only worthwhile diversification) to an investor's portfolio. And worse, investors pay exorbitant fees to get their hands on this kind of dubious diversification.

Chapter 5

The Enemy Within

> "The investor's chief problem—and even his worst enemy—is likely to be himself."
>
> – Benjamin Graham
> Mentor to Warren Buffett

It is easy to read and hear about the studies showing how irrational people can be and say to ourselves, "Of course people are irrational! People are idiots! Not me, though. I'm an exception. This doesn't apply to me." But we should not assume that behavioral biases and irrational quirks do not apply to us just because we are smart or rational most of the time. You are not always on top of your game—no one is—and so there are going to be at least a few times in your life (probably more) when you will not be your best self, and where you may be particularly vulnerable to letting irrational impulses take control.

Behavioral Finance and Economics

Historically, the major theories in finance and economics have been based on the assumption that individuals behave rationally—at all times, in all places, and under all circumstances. This assumption might sound bizarre. After all, everyone knows at least a few people, and probably more, who aren't rational all the time. But academics and theorists clung to this assumption because they needed it to simplify their theories and make all the pieces fit neatly together.

The minority of economists and financial academics who tried to point out the absurdity of this assumption were generally ignored. So, in order to build their case, this brave minority of academics set out to document and categorize as many irrational behaviors as they could find. With enough of these documented, perhaps they thought they could finally blow the old theories out of the water. And so was born the field of *behavioral economics*, and shortly after the field of *behavioral finance*.

Specialists in these fields study individual psychology and group dynamics to understand what motivates people to make financial decisions, ranging from how we choose which grocery store we will frequent to how we choose a stock for our own retirement portfolio. Their research has shown—and continues to show—that *real* people, making *real* decisions, involving *real* money, can and do make irrational decisions all the time. Many of these researchers have even come to see these irrational behaviors as consistent enough to be predictable.

To spare you the labor of reading all the books and research papers on the subject, we will share with you the key findings that are more likely to have an impact on you personally or on those you deal with as you plan your financial future.

"Market tops take a long time to form, and timing is difficult to ascertain because the emotions near the top are greed and hope— longer-lasting emotions. If you buy a stock near a top and see it go down, hope makes you stick with it. Similarly, greed pushes people to buy stocks even near the highs—on the hope for additional gains. On the other hand, market bottoms come with selling climaxes because the associated emotions—fear and anxiety—hurt. You can't sleep. People are faster to throw in the towel."

– Hersh Cohen, Managing Director
ClearBridge Investments, *Barron's* April 2017

The Survival Instinct: Relics from the Hunter-Gatherer

Our most basic instinct is the survival instinct (or the "fight-or-flight response") that evolved to help us hide from predators on plains of Africa,* or defend ourselves during a raid by a rival tribe, or turn and flee from a wooly mammoth hunt gone wrong. Today, however, this instinct has little use. We rarely—if ever—find ourselves in life-or-death situations.

And in the complex world we live in today, getting out of a life-or-death situation would often require more thinking than the survival instinct would allow. It's called the "fight-or-flight" response for a reason. Thought itself is inhibited, and especially any long-range thinking. The survival instinct is about surviving now. It doesn't care about tomorrow, or the next day, or what your life will be like in retirement.

> "Here's a simple, effective way to lower your anxiety: Investors who perceived the least risk were those who checked their investments no more than once a year."
>
> – Richard Thaler, Economist

Unfortunately, evolution has not caught up to the fact that our lives are rarely in danger and long-term thinking has become essential to our success in the modern world. Instead, our neglected survival instinct bursts to the surface whenever it gets the chance. We freeze right before delivering a speech—even though we know we're not going to die. Or worse, we panic and sell our stocks in a

---

* While it's called the "fight-or-flight" response, it's really a fight, flight, or *freeze* response. Our ancient ancestors would freeze when noticing a predator to avoid drawing its attention. This is why today we often find ourselves paralyzed by fear just as often as we feel compelled to fight or flee.

market downturn—even though, on some higher level of consciousness, we know that the risks are actually lower than they were when the same stocks were higher. At any sign of danger, the survival instinct thrusts us into action—to stop the pain *NOW*, regardless of the consequences.

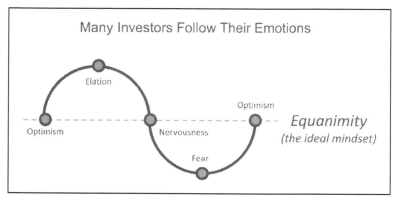

Figure 5-1: Following a reactive cycle of elation and fear can lead to poor decisions at the worst times. Source: Dimensional Fund Advisors and RVW Research.

Herding

Herding is caused by a variety of psychological tendencies, often working together. These include social proof, the fear of missing out (FOMO), mass hysteria, and many others. In all cases, the result is the same: People begin to move and act as though they are one giant mass (or herd) consumed by the same driving emotions, whether fear, euphoria, or something else.

"Most people just can't think about risk in an analytic way. The average person goes by gut feelings."

– Paul Slovic, Professor of Psychology
University of Oregon

It's human nature to want to join in and celebrate the good times with other people, which in the world of investments and finance means buying when the market is rushing upward—and usually near its peak. We saw this with the dotcom bubble. Federal Reserve chairman, Alan Greenspan, noticed something was wrong as early as 1997, when he commented that investors appeared to be driving the market up by the force of their own "irrational exuberance."

> From the animal kingdom, we see that we are genetically programmed to herd when we feel safe and flee when we sense danger. That will lead many to buy at the top and sell into the panic. They pay dearly for that. Suppressing one's instincts is the chief task of equity investors.

The opposite of this irrational exuberance is the mass hysteria that takes hold during a market downturn. Market downturns are a real issue, of course, but once they trigger mass hysteria, they become something else entirely. When the stock market lost half of its value, from the peak in 2007 to the low in 2009, it's not as though the economy itself had lost half of its value. Outside of the financial and real estate sectors, the bulk of the economy continued to function. And we certainly didn't see economic activity itself scale back by 50%—real GDP fell by just 4%. It was the mass hysteria, triggered by the collapse of financial firms, that sent stock prices spiraling so far down. If it's hard to believe that mass hysteria could be so powerful, consider the homier example in the sidebar "Perfume Sickens 144 People" on page 83.

Spotting Bubbles: When the Shoeshine Boys Talked Stocks It Was a Great Sell Signal in 1929

It is said that Joe Kennedy, a famous and wealthy man in his day, exited the stock market in timely fashion after a shoeshine boy gave him some stock tips. He figured that when the shoeshine boys have tips, the market is too popular for his own good, a theory also advanced by Bernard Baruch, another vested interest who described the scene before the big Crash as follows:

> "Taxi drivers told you what to buy. The shoeshine boy could give you a summary of the day's financial news as he worked with rag and polish. An old beggar who regularly patrolled the street in front of my office now gave me tips and, I suppose, spent the money I and others gave him in the market. My cook had a brokerage account and followed the ticker closely. Her paper profits were quickly blown away in the gale of 1929."

Perfume Sickens 144 People

On July 30, 2009, at an office in Fort Worth, Texas, a worker sprayed a small amount of perfume. A nearby coworker complained that the perfume was making her dizzy. This led others to speculate that maybe there was a carbon monoxide leak in the building. As word spread, chaos ensued. In their panicked, hyperventilating states, people began to show psychosomatic symptoms: headaches, dizziness, and even vomiting. In the end, 110 people were treated at the scene, 34 were taken to a hospital, and 12 were taken by ambulance. No carbon monoxide or other toxic fumes were ever found. It all came down to one small puff of perfume and one large episode of mass hysteria.

Recency Bias

People tend to give more weight and significance to their most recent experiences. We tend to think that future experiences will be like the ones from our recent past and not, instead, like the ones from a month or a year ago. We are rarely surprised to see a weather forecast that says tomorrow will be just like today. In the markets, this means we expect the trends we see today to carry on tomorrow. The hard truth is that in the short-term, stock prices move in a completely random pattern (what academics call a "random walk"). When we think we see a trend, it's no different from flipping heads three times in a row and thinking we've got a hot hand. Yet the fact that three heads preceded the fourth flip has no effect whatsoever on the outcome of the fourth flip. The same is true for short-term stock trends.

In the long-term (as we've already discussed), the market does have an overall upward trend, but this is interrupted by sine-wave-like ups and downs that no one can predict. Nonetheless, when we look at a chart trending this way or that, we impute agency and momentum to the line as if it were a deer running through a field. Perhaps this was a helpful skill for our ancestors, who needed to mentally project the path of a deer so they could hit their mark. But seeing agency and momentum where there is none has cost many investors a great deal of money.

> "The biggest mistake investors make is to believe that what happened in the recent past is likely to persist. They assume that something that was a good investment in the recent past is still a good investment. Typically, high past returns simply imply that an asset has become more expensive and is a poorer, not better, investment."
>
> – Ray Dalio, Founder
> Bridgewater Associates

Data Worship

We are constantly becoming more and more datacentric (some might say "data-obsessed") as a society. We assume, without thinking, that a correlation must exist between the amount of data we have and our ability to predict the future. We find ourselves believing that, *given enough data,* we can solve any problem.

> Gathering more data is a poor substitute for thought and analysis—*no matter how good or confident it makes you feel.*

There is a very strong reason for this view, much of which is valid. After all, it worked for the space shuttle. Piles of data make it possible to perform successful heart transplants and minimize organ rejection. Studies and past experience have eliminated guesswork from the construction of bridges, buildings, and other structures essential to modern life.

But the problem comes in when we begin to deify data as a savior in itself. Not all data is equal. Not all of it is even good. Some can be irrelevant and distracting. Still more piles of data may turn out to be unreliable. Like a camper with piles of wood and no match, we sometimes forget the one thing that makes all these piles of raw data worth having. Here, the match that unlocks the value stored in all those piles of data is the capacity of the human mind to process data effectively, and through this make proper inferences and draw proper generalizations.

Do You Really Need More Data?

While working for the CIA, Richards J. Heuer, Jr. tried to answer the question of whether more data results in more accurate predictions. In his paper, "Do You Really Need More Information", he found that more data increased the *confidence* of analysts in their estimates but did not improve their actual accuracy. The results below are for horse racing handicappers whose confidence would go up and up as they were given more data while their accuracy remained unchanged.

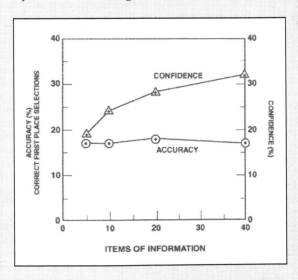

By worshiping "big data", and gathering more of it, we too often create in ourselves a false sense of confidence. We think we have an edge because we have all this data. But if we haven't taken the time to ask questions like, "Is this relevant?" "Is it reliable?" "What does it mean?" "Is that conclusion valid or are there other alternative explanations?" If we're not asking these questions, then we are only fooling ourselves and paving a path to failure.

Market Memory

As creatures with the ability to create, store, and recall memories into the present, we sometimes forget that other creatures do not have memories quite like ours, and we often even impute the capacity for memory into inanimate objects and social phenomena like the market itself. But of course, *the market isn't a person. It has no memory.* Yet one of the most common investor mistakes is to act as though the market has a memory of where a stock price was trading when we bought it. The investors who do this wait for the stock or index to return to this price before selling. But the market does not care, nor even remember, the price you paid. Waiting for the market to go back to where it was out of some consideration for your own circumstances is not so different from having an imaginary friend.

Another common and related mistake is to assume that more cohesive and organized social institution such as the government or corporations have some form of memory. We think to ourselves things like, "Mortgage lenders won't make such bad loans again after the lessons they learned from the housing crisis." But the danger here lies in not understanding how institutional memory differs from individual memory.

"Investing is not a game where the guy with the 160 IQ beats the guy with the 130 IQ . . . once you have ordinary intelligence, what you need is the temperament to control the urges that get other people into trouble in investing."

– Warren Buffett

How well an institution will learn from the past depends on how long people within the institution stay in the same roles they were in when they learned their lessons. If front-line mortgage lenders have been promoted to management positions or changed careers, then the new generation of front-line mortgage lenders may not know what things looked like shortly before the housing crisis. And while the managers may have been front-line lenders during that time, they will now be viewing things from a different vantage point, and they won't know what it was like for managers when they were front-line workers during the last crisis, all making it harder for them to spot any similarities. Thus, institutional memory tends to only last as long as the average length of stay for an employee in a given role within the institution.

"An investor needs to be 'armed with mental weapons that distinguish him in kind—not in a fancied superior degree—from the trading public,' most of whom are short-term-minded speculators. In other words, good investors don't succeed because they are better at guessing what the market will do in the short term; they succeed because they have the mental strength to steer clear of the short-term guessing game and stay focused on value, fundamentals and the long term."

– Benjamin Graham
Mentor to Warren Buffett

Technical Analysis

One issue that's related to data worship and the perception of market memory is what's referred to as "technical analysis."

This is an approach to investing that believes we can predict where stocks are going based on historical patterns. For instance, a "head-and-shoulders" pattern is thought to predict a market decline.

Various patterns of dips, peaks, and pennants are thought to similarly tell us something about the future. In truth, however, this approach is really no more scientific than reading animal entrails to divine the weather. It's more a product of the way our minds work than any underlying reality of the investments.

Warren Buffett has expressed a similar view towards technical analysis:

> "I realized technical stock analysis didn't work when I turned the charts upside down and didn't get a different answer."

And so, too, has author Fred Schwed, Jr.:

> "There has always been a considerable number of pathetic dopes who busy themselves examining the last thousand numbers which have appeared on a roulette wheel, in search of a repeating pattern."

Chapter 6

Diversification

"'Tis the part of a wise man to keep himself today for tomorrow, and not to venture all his eggs in one basket."

– Miguel de Cervantes, Author
Don Quixote

The notion that it's good to diversify goes as far back as the age-old expression: "Don't put all your eggs in one basket." The phrase is so common that we just gloss over it without stopping to consider what it really means. After all, what's so bad about having all your eggs in one basket? To better understand the metaphor, we need to conjure up the image.

If all of our eggs are in one basket, any number of things can happen to cause us to lose all our eggs at once. In the snap of a finger, we can go from having many eggs to having none. We might drop the basket, knock it over, or set it somewhere the dog can reach. Maybe the whole house will burn down, taking the eggs with it. The point is, if we don't spread our eggs around and tuck them into different nooks and crannies, there are countless unpredictable ways to lose them all at once. That's not a chance you want to take.

Figure 6-1: Think of what it means to have all your money in one place.

Beyond Common Sense

While the benefits of diversification have long been a matter of common sense, we should never jump to conclusions based on common sense alone. In life, it's best to follow those ideas which have both the backing of common sense *and* empirical rigor.

Fortunately for us, way back in 1952, a professor of finance at U.C. San Diego, Harry Markowitz, put this common-sense notion to the test. In his seminal paper, *Portfolio Selection*, he used math and his observations of stock price behavior to show quite clearly the empirical truth behind the common sense. He would later win the Nobel Prize in Economics for his work.

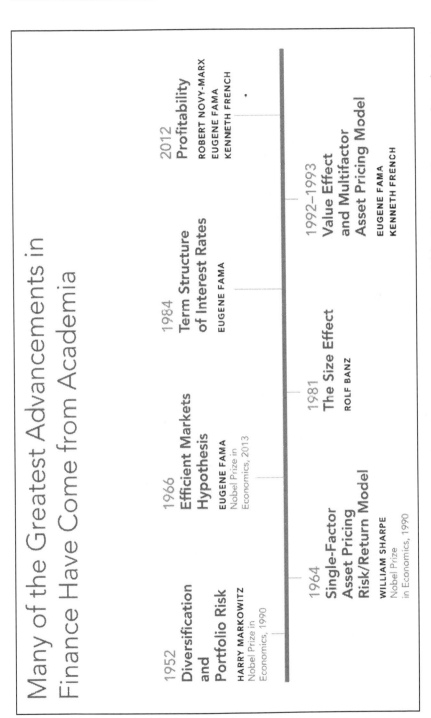

Figure 6-2: From the well-established benefits of diversification to the "value" and "size" effects we'll cover in later chapters, many of the major insights into sound investing have come from academia. Source: Dimensional Fund Advisors.

Markowitz's basic finding was that the meaningless wiggles that individual stocks make during the day largely cancel each other out when many stocks are held together in a portfolio. As one stock would wiggle upward another would wiggle downward. An investor who held a diversified portfolio of such stocks would benefit from synchronous gains (which would come from the persistent growth in the underlying economy) without having to suffer the fits and tantrums of individual stocks along the way.

According to Markowitz's research, the exact amount of risk reduction attained by adding more stocks to a portfolio could be precisely calculated. The results are shown in Table 6-1. As the table shows, almost all of the risk reduction comes from the first 32 stocks. However, that's assuming these first 32 stocks are all perfectly *uncorrelated*, which is never completely the case in reality. And since modern low-cost index fund ETFs (covered in Chapter 9) make it as cheap to own 1,000 stocks as it is to own 32, savvy investors chose to capture the full amount of this category of risk reduction by investing in these types of ETFs.

> "Diversification is the closest thing to a free lunch in investing."
>
> – Harry Markowitz, Nobel Laureate

While Markowitz's paper focused mostly on U.S. stocks, the same logic applies and extends to diversifying across different countries and asset classes (see sidebar "Asset Classes"). Figure 6-3 shows results similar to those in Table 6-1 for the amount of risk reduction that comes from diversifying across asset classes.

Asset Classes

When financial professionals refer to an "asset class" they are referring to the different classifications of investment types. The basic asset classes are stocks, bonds, commodities, and real estate, though there are many others if you include hedge funds, private equity funds, and other investment vehicles as separate asset classes.

It's important to diversify across asset classes because an entire asset class can sometimes be singled out by circumstances and get hit much harder than the others. Bonds, for instance, suffered greatly during the 1980s in part due to high interest rates and the "junk bond" and savings and loan crises that scared investors away from that asset class altogether. Equities suffered a similar fate across the board after the dotcom bubble burst in 2000. To put this in more technical terms, we would say that these different asset classes have low correlations. The correlations are often low enough that people refer to them as being "uncorrelated" or "poorly correlated" as in the following quote:

> "The essence of effective portfolio construction is the use of a large number of poorly correlated assets."
>
> – William J. Bernstein, Financial Theorist and Author
> *The Intelligent Asset Allocator*

Number of Stocks in the Portfolio	Percentage of Risk Eliminated
2	46%
4	72%
8	81%
16	93%
32	96%
64	98%
500	99%
All stocks	100%

Table 6-1: Increasing the number of holdings in a portfolio decreases the overall portfolio risk. Source: Institute for Econometric Research & RVW Research.

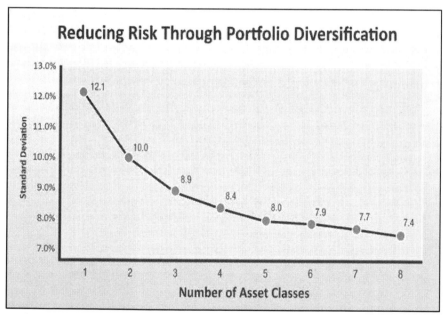

Figure 6-3: Portfolio volatility decreasing as more asset classes are added. The asset classes used in the figure include a variety of stock indexes, various measures of bond performance, and real estate. The risk steadily declines as the portfolio become more diversified. Source: RVW Research

The Case for Diversification
The randomness of the performance of asset classes

	1997	1998	1999	2000	2001	2002	2003	2004	2005	2006	2007	2008	2009	2010	2011	2012	2013	2014	2015	2016
Highest Return	■ 33.4	■ 28.6	★ 29.8	◄ 21.5	★ 22.8	◄ 17.8	★ 60.7	◆ 20.7	◆ 14.0	◆ 26.9	◆ 11.6	◄ 25.9	◆ 32.5	★ 31.3	◄ 27.1	★ 18.2	★ 45.1	◄ 24.7	■ 1.4	★ 25.6
	★ 22.8	◆ 20.3	◆ 27.3	▲ 5.9	▲ 3.8	▲ 1.6	◆ 39.2	★ 18.4	◄ 7.8	★ 16.2	◄ 9.9	▲ 1.6	■ 28.1	◆ 15.1	● 2.9	◆ 17.9	■ 32.4	■ 13.7	▲ 0.0	■ 12.0
	● 15.9	◄ 13.1	■ 21.0	● 0.1	◄ 3.7	● -6.3	■ 28.7	● 11.9	● 7.1	● 15.8	● 5.5	● -17.9	★ 26.5	● 13.0	■ 2.1	■ 16.0	◆ 23.3	● 7.4	◆ -0.4	● 8.2
	◄ 15.9	● 11.9	● 14.8	★ -3.6	● -0.6	◆ -13.3	● 26.2	■ 10.9	★ 5.7	■ 13.0	■ 5.3	■ -36.7	● 14.4	■ 10.1	▲ 0.0	● 11.1	● 17.6	★ 2.9	● -0.6	◄ 1.8
	▲ 5.3	▲ 4.9	▲ 4.7	■ -9.1	■ -11.9	★ -15.7	◄ 1.4	◄ 8.5	■ 4.9	▲ 4.8	▲ 4.7	★ -37.0	▲ 0.1	◄ 8.2	◆ -3.3	▲ 3.4	▲ 0.0	▲ 0.1	◄ -0.7	◆ 1.5
Lowest Return	◆ 2.1	★ -7.3	◄ -9.0	◆ -14.0	◆ -21.2	■ -21.1	▲ 1.0	▲ 1.2	▲ 3.0	◄ 1.2	★ -5.2	◆ -43.1	◄ -14.9	▲ 0.1	★ -11.7	◄ 0.1	◄ -12.8	◆ -4.5	★ -3.6	▲ 0.2

Legend:
- ★ Small stocks
- ■ Large stocks
- ◆ International stocks
- ◄ Long-term government bonds
- ▲ Treasury bills
- ● Diversified portfolio

Figure 6-4: This figure shows us how much it varies from year to year which asset classes do best and which ones do worst. Source: RVW Research.

Devious Deviations

The reduction in portfolio risk shown in Figure 6-2 is represented by the decreasing standard deviation (vertical axis) as more asset classes are added to the portfolio. Specifically, what we are concerned with here is the standard deviation of the portfolio's annual rate of return (often referred to as the portfolio's "volatility"). This measure tells us how much we can expect the results for any given period to deviate from the average return we expect to achieve in the long-run.

You might be wondering why risk is equated with standard deviation (i.e. how much a portfolio's returns wiggle around its average) but there are very good reasons for this.

The first has to do with basic human discomfort and anxiety. When your portfolio's balance is soaring to astronomical heights one day and flirting with zero the next, it's hard to sleep. Be honest with yourself for a moment. In that kind of situation, how can you stop your brain from asking again and again, "What's going on here? How can I make sense of this? What should I do?" Even if you're the calm type, it's hard not to have at least some part of your mind—even in the very back corner—nagging you. This kind of "cognitive load" is what really wears on people.

"A rising tide lifts all boats, but every year some vessels in the stock market spring a leak. Broad diversification ensures they won't sink the whole portfolio."

– Weston Wellington, Vice President
Dimensional Fund Advisors

The second reason is related to the first. We feel anxious when our portfolio is going up and down because *we really can run into problems*. If our portfolio drops close to zero and an emergency strikes, we might be forced to sell our shares to pay a medical bill or a legal settlement we never saw coming. And, in such cases, we don't always have the luxury of waiting for a volatile stock or portfolio to come back to the price we think is right before we need the money. By holding a diversified portfolio, we minimize the chance that we'll find ourselves caught in this kind of lose-lose situation.

Finally, when a stock or an undiversified portfolio has an unusually high volatility, there's often an underlying economic reason. While it's still true that most of the up and down wiggles we see are meaningless, when the swings are especially wide, they often reflect a situation where the people who follow the stocks involved are confused or are otherwise unable to make sense of the circumstances faced by the underlying companies. Just as an example, stock prices are often very volatile for companies that have a lot of debt: One day, when it looks like they'll go bankrupt, the stock price drops close to zero; the next day, when it looks like maybe the company will survive its short-term troubles, the stock price will soar back up. A similar pattern emerges for companies facing fraud allegations and the like. In these cases, there is a real danger that these companies may go bankrupt or otherwise suffer a permanent loss. Then it's no longer about waiting for the wiggles to pass. In such cases, no matter how long you wait, you might still find yourself holding an empty bag.

Before moving on, we should point out that even the volatility of an entire sector can be linked to real underlying economic circumstances (which is why it's important to diversify across sectors). The entire defense sector, for instance, could exhibit volatile price levels for a period of time due to the uncertainty around some pending act by Congress or the President. Or with frauds and accounting manipulation, often problems that emerge for one company turn out to have deeper roots in an accounting loophole or some other oversight that all companies within the same sector can exploit. As a result, if it turns out that the other companies are engaged in the same practices, or if the loop holes are eliminated by new legislation, then the entire sector will likely suffer the consequences. In recognition of the associated sector-wide uncertainty that ensues, the associated stocks will often have a much higher volatility. And so, again, we can see that even when an entire sector is involved, an unusually high standard deviation ("volatility"), can still serve as a good measure of just how much risk we are exposing ourselves to.

Why Banks Use Standard Deviation

Banks use standard deviation to measure risk even though they don't face medical emergencies and the like. They do so because they often use stocks and other securities as collateral for loans they make to hedge funds and other financial institutions.

If the bank requires collateral to cover 80% of a loan and the price of the collateral collapses, the bank will need to force repayment to keep its books in balance and to avoid running afoul of regulators. The borrower, then, often must sell other stocks or securities to repay the loan. These types of knock-on effects are a part of what caused the 2007-2008 financial crisis to spiral downward (on top of the behavioral bias covered in Chapter 5).

We can't all wait for the ups and downs to pass, all at the same time, and waiting forever. Eventually a bank calls a loan, or an emergency strikes, and things start to fall apart. Banks minimize the wiggles so that when things get bad, they don't get *that* bad. Investors minimize the wiggles so that if they get caught in the middle, or if an emergency strikes, their personal lives don't suffer.

Rebalancing

One of the biggest challenges of diversification is that it requires periodic rebalancing to maintain the desired asset allocation. Many investors fail to do this after initially setting up a diversified portfolio, and over time, as one asset class outperforms the others, the portfolio becomes unbalanced. The rising asset class begins to take up a bigger and bigger percentage of the portfolio.

Once that happens, the portfolio begins to take on characteristics such as higher volatility or lower returns that don't match the investor's original plan. Unless the portfolio is periodically and systematically rebalanced, large gains can slowly slip away or investors can end up with a portfolio that they no longer recognize.

> Don't allow the market to decide your asset allocation.

Fortunately for investors, the process of rebalancing indirectly applies the most fundamental rule of investing: buy low and sell high. The portfolio is rebalanced by selling some of the assets that have gone up in value (sell high) while using the proceeds to buy more of the assets that have gone down in value (buy low). This restores the portfolio to the desired allocation percentages while benefitting investors along the way.

Investors should review their holdings with a trusted investment advisor at least once a year or when the asset allocations have drifted more than 5% from their target allocations. Over the course of a year, or even six months, a portfolio that started as 60% stocks and 40% bonds can easily become 50% stocks and 50% bonds, or 70% stocks and 30% bonds. So be sure to pay attention (or make sure your investment advisor is paying attention) and do this rebalancing as recommended. The process itself should be like the kind of periodic tune-up you would do for a car: You're not doing any major redesigns or even changing the paint color. You're still keeping the same basic car, but making a few adjustments here and there to keep things running as smoothly as they did when you first bought the car.

> Equal-weighted indexes (covered in Chapter 9) combine broad market diversification and stock selection with *automatic rebalancing*.

Time and Risk

Another way to reduce risk through diversification is to use time as your ally. The longer you hold your investments, the more the risk and volatility of portfolio returns goes down (see Fig. 6-3). There is always the risk of suffering large *paper* losses during a downturn. But paper losses—the losses that show up in account balances and financial statements—only become real losses when we actually sell the assets at the currently lower prices. Often, if we can hang on long enough, these losses get reversed to gains and more gains as the broader market resumes its upward climb. Having a portfolio that minimizes volatility for a given return and some moral support from a trusted financial advisor will help get you through the lows so that you don't get caught selling into the depths. And, since, all in all, *and over time*, the economy continues to grow, the broad market indexes are much more likely than not to provide a considerable long-term return on your money when compared to other assets. Think of it this way: If you invested in the stock market (by investing in broad-based low-cost index funds like the ones we'll cover in Chapters 7-9), held it for 20 years, and actually managed to lose money, it would be the first time in human history that such a thing had ever happened.

> Time is the friend of the well-constructed portfolio, and the enemy of all others.

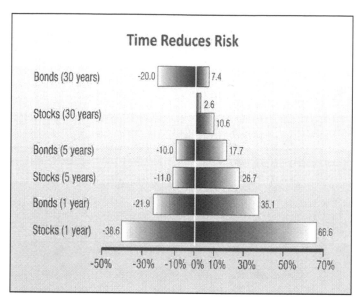

Figure 6-5: The variability of stock returns diminishes over longer time frames. Young people can take advantage of this. Bonds, on the other hand, retain their riskiness. Source: JeremySiegel.com & RVW Research.

The last point we'll make on diversification and its relation to time is that, when suddenly investing or withdrawing very large sums of money, it is almost always wise and prudent to spread out the investment or withdrawal of these sums in smaller chunks across time. This helps to avoid accidentally investing all at once at a high point in the market and selling all at once at a low point in the market. Since it is nearly impossible to predict what the market is going to do in a single day, it is better to not put all of your eggs in one basket chronologically. This approach is referred to as "dollar-cost averaging" and is fairly standard practice. Indeed, it would be an extreme case for an advisor to be unfamiliar with this concept and its beneficial use. Nonetheless, you should know this and keep it in mind for yourself. *Investments ought to be made incrementally over a period, and so should withdrawals be made gradually. In a sense, this is diversification over time.*

Risk vs. Volatility

Diversification is the closest thing investors get to a free lunch. Essentially it replaces risk with volatility. And while volatility can be a good indicator of risk, the two are not identical.

Volatility refers to the wiggles that often have little to no meaning. Most of the time they are just the wild mood swings of Mr. Market (see "Mr. Market" sidebar on page 3).

Risk, on the other hand, refers to the real-world situations investors—or rather *undiversified* investors—should be worried about. These include company risks that impact a single company, such as the BP oil spill, and they also include sector risks, such as a cut to military spending, which would negatively impact the entire defense sector. Diversifying across companies and sectors minimizes these risks, leaving only the third type of risk to contend with: Market risk.

Market risk, however, is only a real-world risk if we are forced to sell at the wrong time. If we can comfortably ride out periods of volatile prices, then this last risk is really no risk at all. In this latter case, we still experience volatility, but not risk.

In all three types of risk, the common feature is the potential for permanent loss. Whether a specific company goes bankrupt, a sector-focused mutual fund goes bust, or you are forced to sell your stocks during a market downturn, you are left holding nothing. These investments are gone, and they will never recover. This is what we want to avoid through diversification and effective planning.

Chapter 7

Indexes Unveiled

> "In the short run, the market is a voting machine
> but in the long run, it is a weighing machine."
>
> – Benjamin Graham

Before we dive into the topic of *index funds*, we should go over the much older *market indexes* that laid the groundwork for index funds and helped shape them into what they are today.

It's common to hear amid the din and clatter of a cocktail party comments like, "The Dow was up a hundred points today", "The NASDAQ down twenty", "The S&P 500 didn't budge!", and so on. But what, on earth, do these monikers mean? As confusing as it all sounds, "the Dow", "the NASDAQ", and "the S&P 500" all refer to different aspects of essentially the same thing: the stock market. The confusion arises because each one refers to a different approach to measuring the market (or in some cases measuring a different segment of the market). These are all what we call stock market indexes.

A stock market index is a basket of stocks that have been chosen because they are thought to be representative of the overall economy or some specific sector. The price of the index is the combined value of its components. In this sense, an index is very much like a measuring device in the medical field. In the field of medicine, if you want to take the temperature of someone's body, you stick a thermometer in their mouth because this will give you a temperature reading that's a pretty good estimate for the entire body. Similarly, if you want to take the "temperature" of the stock market as a whole, you can get a pretty good estimate by taking the "temperature" for a smaller group of representative companies.

Other indexes take this same basic approach but focus more narrowly to take measurements of specific areas of the economy. If you want to check the health of the transportation sector, use a transportation index! If you want to see how the biggest companies are doing, use a "large-cap" index. If you want to see how the smallest companies are doing, use a "small-cap" index.

> "In the long run the stock market indexes fluctuate around the long-term upward trend of earnings per share."
>
> – Sir John Templeton, Fund Manager

The most popular indexes are the "broad-based" indexes, meaning those that attempt to measure the health of the stock market as a whole within a specific country. Typically, they do this by including the largest companies on the largest stock exchanges. In this way, they capture a large chunk of the overall economy without having to track thousands of individual stocks. The Dow Jones Industrial Average (DJIA) and the S&P 500® Index are both broad-based indexes in the United States. Similar indexes provide measures of market activity in other countries. Examples include the FTSE 100 in Britain, the CAC 40 in France, the DAX in Germany, the Nikkei 225 in Japan, the Sensex in India, and the Hang Seng Index in Hong Kong.

Other than broad-based indexes, there are also specialized indexes that track the performance of specific sectors. For example, before there was the Dow Jones *Industrial* Average, there was the

Dow Jones *Transportation* Average, which consisted of twenty companies exclusively in the transportation sector, such as railroad and trucking companies. Other indexes are even more specialized: The American Stock Exchange Interactive Week Internet Index (that's a mouthful!) tracks the stock of forty-two companies that sell products and services related to the Internet.

Over time, indexes have become so popular and integral to financial activities (including their use in financial contracts and for measuring the performance of fund managers) that they have become valuable in their own right. This is why they are often trademark protected, and reported and owned by individual companies. The DJIA and the S&P 500® indexes, for instance, are both controlled by S&P Global Inc. (formerly known as "McGraw Hill Companies").

The Dow Jones Industrial Average

The Dow Jones Industrial Average (also referred to as the DJIA, Dow 30, or, informally, the Dow Jones, or simply, "the Dow") was created in 1896 by *Wall Street Journal* editor, and Dow Jones & Company co-founder, Charles Dow. Mr. Dow compiled the index as a way to gauge the industrial performance of the US economy. It is the second oldest U.S. stock market index after the Dow Jones *Transportation* Average.

Today, the DJIA consists of thirty of the largest and most widely held public companies in the United States. The "industrial" part of the name is mostly a historical artifact, since most of the companies in the index today are no longer in heavy industry. The "average" in this case is what's called a "price-weighted" average, meaning each stock has an effect on the index proportional to its price relative to the sum of all the component prices. It is also called a "scaled average" because over the years, as there have been stock splits and other technical changes* made to the component stocks, the average has been adjusted by a "divisor" so that the index's price level immediately before a stock split (or some other technical change) matches the index's price level immediately after.

When the DJIA was first published in May 1896, it included just twelve stocks and stood at 40.94. The number of stocks was increased to twenty in 1916, and to thirty in 1928. The component stocks have been changed at irregular intervals under the discretion of the Dow Jones Company, and have changed forty-eight times since 1896. The last such change was on March 19, 2015 when AT&T was replaced by Apple.

Adjusting the Dow

When a price-weighted index is first launched, the "divisor" is simply the number 1, since there would have been no time for anything to happen that would require adjustment. Over time, with all the technical changes that have happened to the Dow's constituent companies, the divisor was down to 0.132 in September 2011. With a divisor less than one, the value of the index is much higher than what we would get from simply summing the component stock prices.

The S&P 500® Index

The S&P 500® index is based on five hundred large-cap, public companies that trade on one of the two major U.S. stock exchanges: the New York Stock Exchange (NYSE) and the

---

* What we mean by "technical changes" are changes that have nothing to do with the value of the underlying company. Stock splits are a good example of this, where suddenly the number of shares outstanding doubles on paper, even though nothing has really changed at the underlying company.

NASDAQ. After the Dow Jones Industrial Average, the S&P 500® is the most widely watched index of U.S. stocks.* Given its large swath of companies, it is often used as a benchmark to gauge the performance of mutual fund managers. If the managers fail to outperform the index, they are seen as adding no value to the investment process.

The index, when it was launched on March 4, 1957, was considered a major technological advance. For the first time ever, thanks to advances in computer technology, a broad-based index with as many as 500 different stocks could be continuously calculated, updated, and distributed in real time. Since its launch, the index has been extrapolated all the way back to 1923, allowing us to use it to gauge the performance of stocks since that time.

The stocks that make up the S&P 500® are selected by a committee, and are selected on the basis of being representative of one of the various industries in the U.S. economy. Together, these 500 companies represent roughly 80% of the total value of stocks that can be traded on public exchanges in the U.S. While this might sound remarkable given that there are more than 4,000 companies listed on the NYSE and NASDAQ exchanges, this results from the fact that the largest 500 companies on these exchanges are much, much larger than the companies that aren't in the S&P 500®.

The S&P 500® Index is what's called a market-cap weighted index, meaning the price of each stock is multiplied by the number of shares outstanding to get what's called the company's "market capitalization" or "market cap." The market cap for each company is then be divided by the total market cap for all the companies in

---

* The S&P 500® includes a handful of non-U.S. companies. However, the index is designed to reflect the value of businesses in the U.S., and so these exceptions are typically cases where a company is incorporated overseas for tax-related or other technical reasons.

the index to determine the proportional representation for each stock in the index. As a result, this approach gives larger companies a bigger influence on the index and smaller companies less influence. On August 8, 2017, based on the share prices of the various companies that day, the ten largest companies made up 20.5% of the total market cap for the entire index. That means the influence of those ten companies, due to the market-cap weighting methodology, would cover 20.5% of the index. Under an equal-weighting methodology (which we will cover in Chapter 9), each company would have a 1/500th (0.2%) such that the ten companies would have a greatly reduced influence of just 2%.

If You Put a Stock in Water, Will It Float?

Technically, the S&P 500® is what's called a "float-weighted" index, which is almost the same as a cap-weighted index, but where the stock price is multiplied by the number of shares available for trading instead of the raw number of shares outstanding. This number is known as the "float", as in the number of shares that are actually floating around out there in the marketplace. This removes the kind of shares that tech companies like to issue to their employees, since these typically can't be traded until some amount of time has passed. The S&P 500® only recently switched from a pure cap-weighted index to a float-weighted index in hopes that it would reduce the chances of another tech bubble.

The NASDAQ

The NASDAQ Composite Index is a market-cap-weighted index comprised of all the stocks listed on the NASDAQ (National Association of Securities Dealers Automated Quotation System) stock exchange—which currently has 2,895 components.

NASDAQ is commonly seen as an indicator of the

performance of technology and growth stocks. However, this is more by coincidence than design. When the exchange was first started in 1971, it used the most cutting-edge technology of the time to create an exchange that was 100% computer-based. The NASDAQ had no trading floor like the one at the New York Stock Exchange, where traders would shout out orders and trade using hand signals.

> "Of all the ways to invest money, ownership of profitable businesses has proved to be the optimal means of creating wealth. The rich do it; so can you. Indeed, investors have reaped greater profits by buying stock in corporate America than by lending out their money or by purchasing real estate and other hard assets. There is no reason to believe that stocks offer less opportunity today. In fact, you may have a tough time reaching your financial goals if you choose to avoid them."
>
> – Anne Farrelly, Author
> *Invest Without Stress*

The large blue-chip companies preferred to stick with the NYSE because they were familiar with it and there was no real reason to switch. Newer tech companies, on the other hand, were eager to embrace the NASDAQ's tech-forward approach, and so they actually preferred to be listed on the NASDAQ. At the same time, smaller companies going public for the first time (which tend to be growth stocks) found it easier to list on the NASDAQ than the NYSE because the computer-based automation allowed the NASDAQ to charge lower listing fees.

The Russell Indexes

Yet another group of indexes is published by Russell Investments. In 1984, Russell recognized that the existing indexes, such as the DJIA and S&P 500®, did not represent the investments that most managers were making. The indexes were flawed (or biased) in a way that explained the inability of active managers to beat the market. The company developed new rules-based indexes to better measure the performance of what they termed "investable stocks." Their goal was to create a series of indexes that could be used as the basis for comparing the returns of mutual funds and other financial products.

Russell has been very successful in getting many mutual funds, ETFs, and futures contracts to track themselves against the Russell indexes. Russell has also created numerous indexes for global markets, and claims that more money is indexed using their benchmarks than any other index family.

Russell's main U.S. stock index is the Russell 3000® index, which includes the leading 3,000 stocks in the U.S. as measured by market cap. The largest 1,000 of those companies are used to construct the large-cap Russell 1000® index, and the remaining 2,000 smaller companies are used to construct the small-cap Russell 2000® index.

The Russell Global® Index reflects the performance of nearly 11,000 stocks worldwide, including the Russell 3000® to represent its U.S. component and the Russell/Nomura Total Market Index as the Japanese component. Russell also publishes value and growth subsets for each of its U.S. indexes. This divides each index approximately in half, separating companies into either the "value" or "growth" category. (The differences between value and growth stocks will be covered in Chapter 9).

The Large and Unlisted

Some of the largest companies in the U.S. do not list their shares on the major U.S. stock exchanges. As a result, these companies are not included in any of the major stock market indexes. One way to get around this is to use the Fortune 500® index, which follows the 500 largest U.S. companies based on gross revenue.

Chapter 8

Index Funds

"Most of the mutual fund investments I have are index funds."

– Charles Schwab, Investor and Financial Executive, Founder of the Charles Schwab Corporation.

Though stock market indexes have been around since the late 1800s, it didn't occur to fund managers to take the same basic concept of stock market indexes and use it to construct index funds that investors could actually trade in. This didn't happen until 1975 when John Bogle, founder of the Vanguard Group, presented this radical idea (or at least it was radical at the time) to his board of directors. Before that time, if you wanted to build a portfolio that would follow the Dow, for example, you would have had to do it yourself, paying higher fees and doing your own rebalancing along the way.

From the very outset of founding his firm, Bogle was obsessed with the idea of creating a new breed of low-cost mutual funds. Instead of trying to "beat" the market through the dubious methods of stock-picking and market-timing, his new fund would attempt to duplicate the performance of the Standard & Poor's 500® Index by purchasing and holding each one of its 500 stocks. The goal was to match, as closely as possible, the market's performance as measured by the S&P, and he believed it could be accomplished by allocating the fund's assets to the component stocks of the Index itself.

Since the choice of stocks to include in the portfolio was already taken care of, the fund would need only a small amount of manpower and resources to periodically update the fund to match the index. And such updating would require only a few trades at a time, resulting in lower trading commissions. This would make it much easier and cheaper to manage than any actively traded fund, earning this investment approach the name "passive" investing. Though, as pointed out in the following quote, this is a bit of a misnomer.

> "Passive investing is a misnomer. Index investors eschew market-timing and stock-picking not out of laziness or passivity, but because those activities usually reduce returns and increase risks. A better name for it would be 'Intelligent Investing.'"
>
> – David M. Blitzer, Chairman
> Standard & Poor Index Committee

Further, with the massive scale of the funds Bogle was creating, they would be able to negotiate rates on trades and commissions that would be cheaper than what an individual investor would get on his or her own trying to recreate the same portfolio from scratch. It would be a true win-win for everyone: the fund, the fund's investors, and the fund's broker (who would gladly accept lower fees in exchange for the large volume of trades that would come from having a large fund as a customer). The only losers, of course, would be the active fund managers, since, if everything went as Bogle planned, they would no longer be able to justify their own existence.

"If you pay the executives at Sarah Lee more, it doesn't make the cheesecake less good. But with mutual funds, it comes directly out of the batter."

– Don Phillips, President
Morningstar, Inc.

By simply lowering expenses, Bogle believed his index funds could outperform actively managed funds:

"I projected the costs of managing an index fund to be 0.3% per year in operating expenses and 0.2% per year in transaction costs. Since fund annual costs at that time appeared to be about 2.0%, I concluded that an index fund should reasonably be expected to provide an annual return of 1.5% above a managed fund."

Fortunately for us, and any investors who care to take notice, time has proven, again and again, his thesis to be correct—*even beyond even his own expectations*. During the 1990s, the gap between actively managed mutual funds and the S&P 500® widened to more than double the 1.5% figure Bogle had predicted, reaching a staggering 3.4% per year.

"There are three classes of people who do not believe that markets work: the Cubans, the North Koreans, and active managers."

– Rex Sinquefield, Co-Founder
Dimensional Fund Advisors

Lagging Behind

Few actively managed funds have kept pace with market indexes in recent years, new data show.

Percentage of U.S. equity funds outperformed by benchmark

Fund category Comparison index	5-year	10-year	15-year
Large-Cap S&P 500	88%	85%	92%
Mid-Cap S&P MidCap 400	90%	96%	95%
Small-Cap S&P SmallCap 600	97%	96%	93%

Note: Data as of Dec. 31, 2016
Source: S&P Dow Jones Indices   THE WALL STREET JOURNAL.

Figure 8-1: Over, 5-, 10-, and 15-year periods, actively managed equity funds consistently underperformed their benchmarks, whether large-cap, mid-cap, or small-cap.

Bogle attributes this large difference in performance between passive and active funds to four factors: 1) expenses, 2) turnover, 3) sector chasing, and 4) cash reserves.

Expenses

The expenses that the average actively managed fund consumed in the 1990s averaged about 1.3% of the money invested in the fund. From Bogle's analysis of the data, he concluded that this alone explained more than a third of the underperformance by active (non-index) funds. For the sake of comparison, the current expenses for Vanguard's S&P 500 index fund are as low as 0.04%. Remarkably, despite the high fees and underperformance of mutual funds in the 1990s, they actually kept *increasing* their fees throughout the decade.

> "Properly measured, the average actively managed dollar must underperform the average passively-managed dollar, net of costs. Empirical analyses that appear to refute this principle are guilty of improper measurement."
>
> – William F. Sharpe
> Nobel Laureate in Economics

While the difference between 1.3% and 0.04%—a mere 1.26%—might not sound like much, these costs can really add up once you factor in the effects of compounding. If we assume a 5% annual return before fees are deducted, this 1.26% difference in fees can result in a 44% difference in the size of your nest egg thirty years later. In forty years, the difference would be 62%. To put it more concretely, imagine we have two funds that make the exact same investments and, therefore, have the exact same performance *before* fees. If they both have an annual return 5% before fees over a 40-year period, a $1,000 investment in the fund that takes out an extra 1.26% in fees would grow to $4,277 compared to $6,934 (62% more) for the fund that does not take out these extra fees. And, bear in mind, this is without considering the three other factors that explain the rest of the 3.4% gap.

> "[T]he mutual fund industry, in particular, is not only an industry where you don't get what you pay for. It turns out—examine the data—you get precisely what you don't pay for. And therefore, if you pay nothing, you get everything."
>
> –John C. Bogle to Steve Forbes,
> *Forbes*, January 2009

Turnover: How "Active Managers" Earn That Title

In pursuit of market-beating returns, active managers tend to buy and sell their holdings at a rapid pace. It's hard for them to resist, since after all, they are getting paid to "do something!" They are also often measured by their short-term performance, which means they don't often give their stocks a chance to show long-term results. The general investor population is full of people with short-term memories, and the marketing departments and compensation committees at the fund managers' firms all know this. The natural consequence of this is that fund managers are pressured to do whatever it takes to have a good month, quarter, or year. As Bogle explains in his 2015 book, *Bogle on Mutual Funds*, the cost of this frenetic trading activity can consume an additional 0.5%–2.0% of return every year.

In contrast, the annual turnover for an index fund is typically 5% or less. As a result, the cost to shareholders of the underlying trading activities can be less than 0.1%. The difference of 0.6% per year increases the wealth of the investor rather than those employed at trading desks at mutual fund firms.

The other piece of this is that the higher turnover of active funds means investors in these funds incur taxes on their gains at higher tax rates. Because of the higher turnover, a greater proportion of the trades take place in too short a time frame to qualify for the lower capital gains tax rates. Index funds, on the other hand, with such low turnover, end up holding the vast majority of their shares long enough for the gains (i.e. your income from these gains) to qualify for the lower rates.

It's not the money you make that counts; it's the money you keep.

Being Active in Passive Funds is *Still* Active

Active funds tend to underperform passive index funds largely due to the costs of active trading within the funds themselves. However, investors in passive index funds can create the same problem for themselves by actively jumping in and out of the underlying passive index funds.

DALBAR's Quantitative Analysis of Investor Behavior (QAIB) report estimates the actual returns experienced by investors compared to the returns of the underlying funds they are investing in. While it seems as though these two numbers should be identical, they can differ precisely because of these in-and-out effects, jumping in and out at just the wrong times.

The QAIB report for 2016 found that the average equity mutual fund investor earned just 7.26% in 2016 compared to 11.96% for the S&P 500® (a 4.70% gap). Similarly, the 20-year annualized return for the average equity mutual fund investor was just 4.79% compared to 7.68% for the S&P 500® (a 2.89% gap).

Sector Chasing

Since active managers are in a constant state of frantically looking for winning stocks, they often turn to some big-picture theory to crease a false sense of order in the outside world and inside their own cluttered heads. This leads them to make the same mistake individual investors make when they chase yesterday's winners, but they do it instead on the sector level. They usually end up making market-lagging bets in the sectors of the economy that did well last quarter. These sector bets hold down returns and partly explain why active management overwhelmingly fails to beat index funds.

> "The stock market is a chaotic hive of millions of people who overpay for hope and underpay for value."
>
> – Jason Zweig, Columnist, *Wall Street Journal*
> "The Intelligent Investor"

Cash Reserves

The fourth factor that hurts actively managed funds is cash reserves. Managers must hold cash reserves to meet shareholder redemption requests. Many also choose to hold even more cash than needed for redemptions because they believe that they can time the market. Holding a portion of clients' portfolios as non-performing cash reserves can be a very expensive practice. This decision made by most fund managers explains a significant part of the underperformance between mutual funds and the market.

> "The best way to own common stocks is through an index fund."
>
> – Warren Buffett

Follow the Leader

Other mutual fund management companies noticed the success that Bogle and Vanguard Group's low-cost index funds enjoyed and began responding by offering their own index funds. There are now funds to match mid-cap indexes, small-cap indexes, small-cap growth indexes, small-cap value indexes, foreign indexes, as well as variations on all of these and many other indexes. Each of these other types of index funds also outperform most managed funds.

"A blindfolded monkey throwing darts at a newspaper's financial pages could select a portfolio that would do just as well as one carefully selected by experts."

– Burton G. Malkiel, Professor of Economics
A Random Walk Down Wall Street

Déjà Vu? Three Decades of Index Superiority—Twice

In 2016, John Bogle took a look back in time to see how the performance of actively managed funds compared to that of the S&P 500® during two 30-year periods. Here's what he found:

	1945–1975		1985–2015	
	Average Equity Fund	S&P 500	Average Large-Cap Fund	S&P 500
Annualized return	9.70%	11.30%	9.60%	11.20%
Index advantage	—	1.60%	—	1.60%
Cumulative return	1539%	2402%	1548%	2494%
Index advantage	—	863%	—	946%

Table 8-1: Active funds have consistently outperformed the S&P 500 over 30-year periods. Source: *Financial Analysts Journal*, Jan/Feb 2016.

Chapter 9

Beyond Traditional Indexes: Moving from Good to Better

"Most indexes are hard-wired to overlook bargains and overpay for wildly popular stocks."

– Joel Greenblatt, Gotham Capital

As we saw in the previous chapter, the major benefit of index fund investing comes from the cost reductions that allow us to escape "the tyranny of compounding costs". While Jack Bogle first did this by mimicking the most popular headline indexes of the day, there are many other ways to construct an index where the process can be automated (making management fees almost nothing) and that involve making only minor periodic adjustments such that transaction fees stay low. In other words, we can take Bogle's key insight and the associated benefits and extend (and even amplify) them beyond the plain vanilla index funds of yesteryear.

The index funds Bogle first created were largely cap-weighted index funds because they were designed to mirror the most popular stock market indexes, most of which are cap-weighted. But since then, various types of index funds have emerged that take different approaches to selecting and weighting the stocks they hold. Some, such as equal-weighted and fundamental-weighted indexes have an advantage over their cap-weighted cousins. As if by accident, the modifications that these funds make to achieve their desired weightings tends to eliminate and even reverse the wealth-inhibiting biases that cap-weighted funds have towards large-cap and fad stocks. For example, equal weighted indexes' automated algorithms effectively force their funds to buy low and sell high, keeping them in line with the most fundamental rule of investing. As a result, they are more diversified and tend to produce larger and more stable returns over time.

Investing in an S&P 500® index allocates around 50% of the funds to the largest 50 companies, and the smallest 50 companies get 2%. The fund is therefore consistently heavily skewed towards the overpriced and favored companies, and underweighted to the underpriced and out-of-favor ones. It is essentially a large-cap growth stock portfolio.

Cap-Weighted Index Funds

The core problem with the more traditional and popular cap-weighted index funds is that, as investing fads gain steam, the index becomes top-heavy with the stocks that, through their faddish popularity, have become overvalued. This comes at the expense of underweighting lower-valued stocks—which are the ones most likely to perform best in the future. The result is that cap-weighted index funds tend to underperform the index funds with weightings that don't move in tandem with the rise and fall of fad stocks. These other weighting schemes include equal-, value-, and small-cap-weighted indexes.

Cap-Weighting: The Hazard of Most Indexes

In a move that rippled across the stock market, on Tuesday, April 5, 2011, Nasdaq OMX announced a rare rebalancing of its NASDAQ-100 index, which reduced the big weighting of Apple, Inc. At the time, the company made up more than 20% of the index. The rebalancing was driven in part by the seemingly unstoppable rise in Apple shares, which were up more than fourfold in the two prior years.

The tech company's big weighting meant that changes in fortune of the maker of iPhones, iPods and iPads would have a huge impact on one of the most heavily traded indexes in the market. In total, 81 of the 100 constituents of the index saw their share of the index increased in the rebalancing.

Equal-Weight Index Funds

The main benefit of equal-weighted index funds is that they remove the biases toward fad stocks and large-cap stocks that occur in cap-weighted index funds. At the same time, they typically provide the same kind of broad exposure we get from cap-weighted indexes by investing in the same exact list of companies that we would find in the popular cap-weighted indexes like S&P 500®. A typical equal-weighted S&P 500® index, for example, would buy stock of each of the 500 companies included in the S&P 500® index, but would do so in equal dollar amounts across the board.

As an added bonus, equally-weighted indexes tend to have lower volatility (risk) than cap-weighted indexes. This is because equal-weighting reduces the risk that the index fund will become overly concentrated in just a few of the fund's holdings. This is what was happening with Apple's influence on the NASDAQ-100 index, as discussed in the sidebar at the top of this page.

Equal-weighted index funds are periodically rebalanced to

maintain their equal weighting, which results in a more consistently broad exposure across the various sectors of the economy, the different sizes of companies, and other diverse company characteristics. If Apple were included in an equal-weighted S&P 500® index, it would make up just one-five-hundredth (0.2%) of the portfolio, preventing it from pushing the fund towards an overconcentration in the tech sector, large-cap companies, and perhaps even an overconcentration in companies with stock prices driven by fads or other forms of psychological momentum.

Look at Figure 9-1 to see the results of this approach. By frequently rebalancing the index fund to maintain equal weighting (thereby preventing one sector from dominating the index) the equal-weighted fund provides larger and steadier returns over time.* Over the eight years following the financial crisis, the equal-weighted index provided an additional 2.64% per year on average. In dollar terms, a $10,000 investment in a traditional cap-weighted index would have increased to about $38,000 over the eight years ending February 2017. That same investment in an equal-weighted index would have grown 19% larger, to more than $45,000. That's an impressive gain for something so seemingly inconsequential as changing the weighting of an index fund.

> Equal-weighted indexing provides automatic rebalancing and is an inherently contrarian strategy.

---

* Note that when we say "frequently rebalancing" here, we are still talking about a tiny amount of trading compared to the frenzied trading of an actively managed fund.

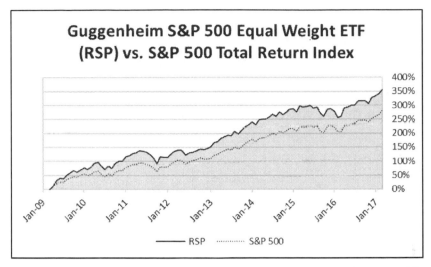

Figure 9-1: An equal-weighted index delivers higher returns in this example. This figure demonstrates the value of buying low and selling high, which is the rebalancing discipline followed by equal-weighted indexes. Source: RVW Research.

Small-Cap Index Funds

Just like equal-weighted index funds, small-cap index funds counteract the destructive large-cap bias found in traditional market-cap-weighted indexes. They do this by forcing managers to hold only small-cap stocks in the index: As the price of a stock rises, moving it up and out of the "small-cap" category, the manager is forced to sell the stock and reinvest in stocks that have fallen back into the "small-cap" category (buy low, sell high).

Compared to an equal-weighted index, this is like going one step further. The equal-weighted index fund says, in effect, "No! We will not let large-caps dominate and hold us back!" The small-cap index fund goes even further to say, "No! We will not let large-caps dominate—in fact, we won't let them in at all!" By going the extra mile to focus exclusively on small-cap stocks, these index funds allow the investors who can stomach the higher volatility associated with small-cap stocks to benefit from the historically higher returns that come with taking on that risk.

As shown in Figure 9-2, over the long term, small-cap stocks have outperformed large-cap stocks by an average of 1.51% annually on a total return basis. In dollar terms, a $1 investment in small-cap stocks would have returned an average of 11.67% and grown to $20,544 over the ninety-year period ending 2016. That same $1 invested in large-cap stocks instead would have grown to just $6,031, an average annual return of 10.16% per year.

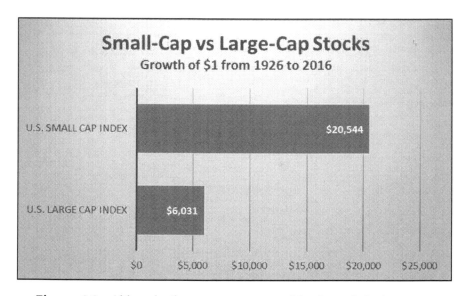

Figure 9-2: Although they carry greater risk than their large-cap counterparts, investments made in small-cap stocks have rewarded investors handsomely in the long run. Source: RVW Research.

Global Index Funds

Global index funds are similar to small-cap index funds in terms of how an investor should think about them. Like a small-cap index fund, a global index fund will tend to be riskier, but in exchange for producing better expected returns. In this way, an investor can use a global index fund to fine-tune his or her portfolio to better match the investor's risk-return profile. Global index funds also have the side-benefit of adding another layer of diversification.

Most investors should consider holding a broad-based index investment in U.S. stocks as their primary, core equity investment within their portfolio. This alone still provides a great deal of diversification. Sometimes it represents the only equity exposure for an individual investor, and that may be adequate for some. But individuals have typically done better by adding international index-based investments into the mix. But even here, we need to make sure we are sticking with low-cost index funds and pay attention to what kind of weighting (market, equal, small-cap, etc.) is being used for the international or global index.

Figure 9-3: The United States makes up 54% of the market in exchange-traded stocks, but when taken together, the opportunity represented by Non-U.S. markets is about the same in size. Source: Dimensional Fund Advisors.

European, Asian, and developing markets are individually much smaller than the U.S. market. But as we can see in Figure 9-3, as a whole, these markets represent an investment opportunity almost as large as the U.S. market. These markets also include some of the best-known global brands (See Table 9-1).

Company Name	Based In
BP (gasoline)	London, England
Samsung (consumer electronics)	Seoul, South Korea
ING (insurance, financial services)	Amsterdam, Netherlands
Adidas (athletic footwear, clothing)	Herzogenaurach, Germany
Rolex (watches)	Geneva, Switzerland
L'Oreal (cosmetics)	Clichy, France
Sony (electronics & entertainment)	Tokyo, Japan
Bayer (pharmaceuticals)	Leverkusen, Germany
Toyota (automobiles)	Toyota City, Aichi, Japan
Barclays (financial services)	London, England
Ikea (Home Furnishings)	Leiden, Netherlands
Nestle (Food, Beverage, Pharma)	Vevey, Switzerland

Table 9-1: Global companies that produce many of the best-known products are a required part of a well-diversified portfolio.

When we look at the data on actual returns, the smaller markets have often done better than the U.S. market. Figure 9-4 shows that over a nineteen-year period, "emerging markets" (represented by the iShares MSCI Emerging Markets fund) had a total return that was nearly 20% higher than the total return for large-cap, U.S.-based stocks (represented by the SPDR S&P 500 fund). The data also shows, in Table 9-2, that developed markets — those developed enough to no longer be considered emerging markets — also provide returns that are often better than the U.S.

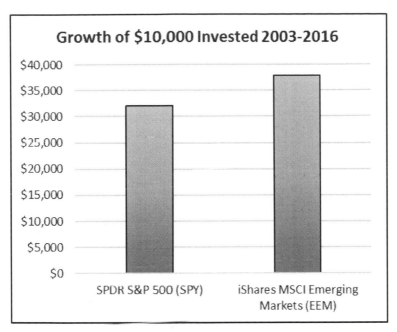

Growth of $10,000 Invested 2003-2016

Figure 9-4: Emerging markets offer greater returns and greater risks to US investors. Again, we see that investors willing and able to bear risk are usually rewarded over time. Source: RVW Research.

Year	U.S. Growth	Best Developed Market Growth	Best Developed Market
2007	5%	49%	Australia
2008	-38%	-29%	Japan
2009	26%	87%	Norway
2010	15%	34%	Sweden
2011	1%	14%	Ireland
2012	15%	40%	Belgium
2013	32%	46%	Finland
2014	13%	13%	United States
2015	1%	23%	Denmark
2016	11%	25%	Canada

Table 9-2: Only once in the past 10 years has the United States been the leading developed market in terms of investment returns. In fact, the returns from well-developed economies often dwarf US stocks. Source: RVW Research.

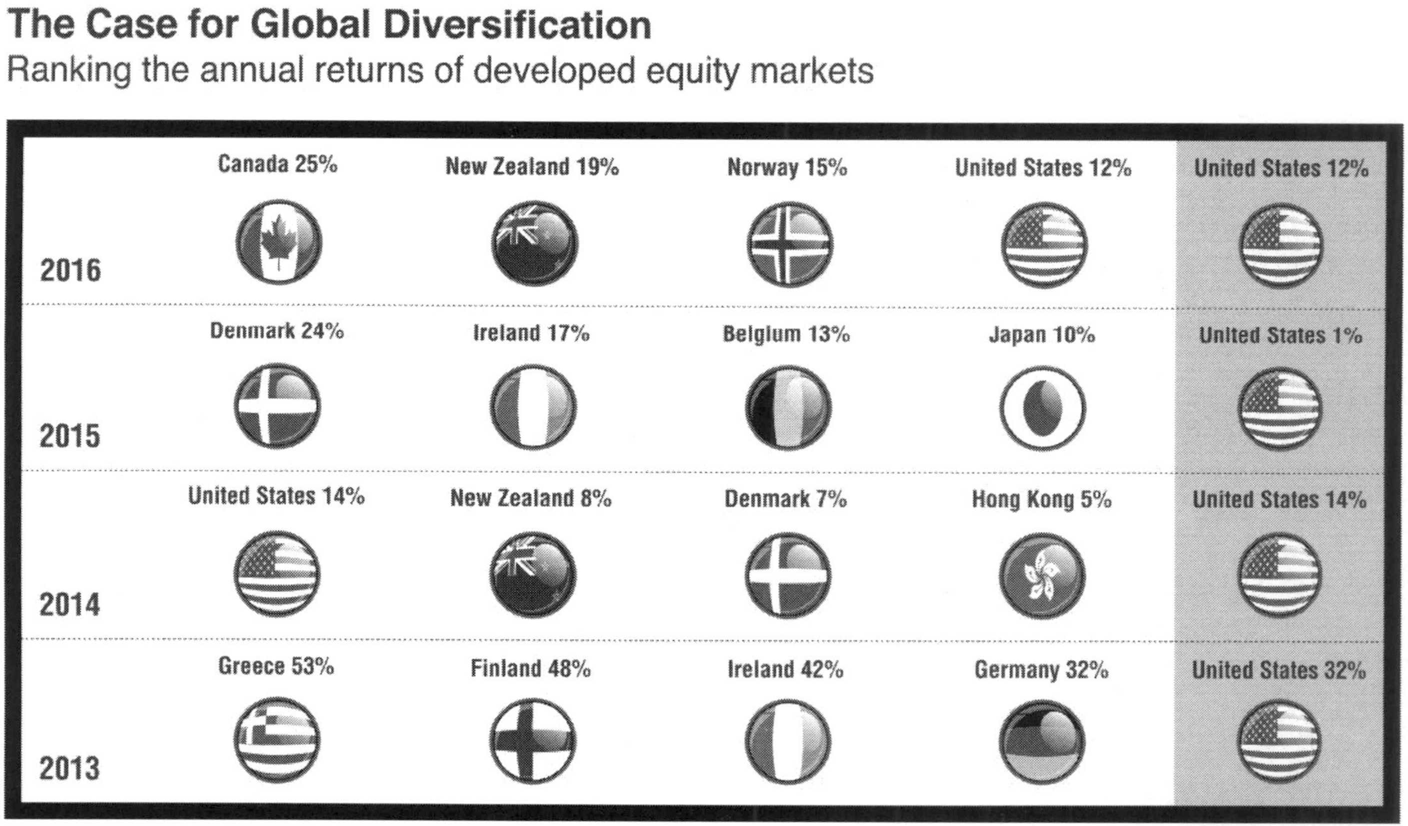

The Case for Global Diversification
Ranking the annual returns of developed equity markets

Figure 9-5: While there are times when the U.S. equity market is the best performing market among developed nations, most of the time this is not the case and some other developed market does much better. Source: RVW Research.

The good thing about adding global investments to a portfolio is that, while you get better returns by taking on more risk, some of this added risk is offset by the lower correlation between these investments and the other investments in the portfolio. In other words, you're confronted with the same basic risk-return tradeoffs involved in adding small-cap stocks to a portfolio (which is appropriate for fine-tuning), but you also get a sweetener on the back end when you consider these investments in the context of a full portfolio.

WHY NOT JUST INVEST IN THE S&P 500®?

	Large-Cap S&P 500	Mid-Cap S&P 400	Small-Cap S&P 600	Emerging Markets	International MSCI EAFE
2000	-9.10%	17.51%	11.80%	-30.61%	-13.95%
2001	-11.89%	-0.60%	6.54%	-2.37%	-21.21%
2002	-22.10%	-14.51%	-14.63%	-6.00%	-15.64%
2003	28.68%	35.62%	38.79%	56.27%	39.16%
2004	10.88%	16.48%	22.65%	25.95%	20.70%
2005	4.91%	12.56%	7.68%	34.54%	14.02%
2006	15.79%	10.32%	15.12%	32.59%	26.86%
2007	5.49%	7.98%	-0.30%	39.78%	11.63%
2008	-37.00%	-36.23%	-31.07%	-53.18%	-43.06%
2009	26.46%	37.38%	25.57%	79.02%	32.46%
Total Return	-9.12%	85.30%	85.17%	161.95%	17.00%
Annualized	-0.95%	6.36%	6.35%	10.11%	1.58%

Table 9-3: Many consider 2000-2009 "the lost decade" for stocks, and indeed it was for the S&P 500® (shown as "Large-Cap S&P 500" in the figure). However, Mid-Cap, Small-Cap, Emerging Markets, and International index-based approaches provided attractive returns. Source: RVW Research.

Fundamental-Weighted Index Funds

There are two general investment styles: value and growth. These two styles dominate the fund industry and account for a large part of stock market trading. Value investors look for stocks that they believe are trading at less than their intrinsic values, selecting those with lower-than-average price-to-book or price-to-earnings ratios, or which may offer high dividend yields. Growth investors look for stocks that they believe will experience a great deal of growth in the future and typically trade at far higher multiples of earnings. Often this is based on a view that the underlying company's earnings will grow at a rate faster than its competitors and the earnings rate for market as a whole.

Fundamental-weighted indexes try to automate this selection process for growth or value stocks by using an algorithm that looks at the "fundamentals" (hence the name) of the underlying companies. Often this involves pulling numbers from their financial statements and other SEC filings.

> Fundamental indexing seeks to assemble groups of companies by looking at the true economic footprint of each company in the same way that one would look at a business one is contemplating buying.

An example of this kind of approach is a proprietary method created by Research Affiliates (based in Newport Beach, CA) that does the weighting of the stocks within an index based on their estimate of the economic footprint of the underlying companies. A variety of accounting figures are used, including sales, dividends, cash flows, and book value. As we can see in Table 9-4, focusing on some of these key attributes can lead to significantly better returns beyond what one would earn from investing in an index that does not take these into account.

	Growth of $1 from 1962-2006	Annual Return	Annual Volatility
S&P 500	$85	10.4%	14.7%
High dividend yield	$166	12.0%	13.4%
Low price-to-book ratio	$177	12.2%	14.6%
Low price-to-cash flow ratio	$207	13.0%	14.5%
Low price-to-sales ratio	$204	12.6%	15.5%

Table 9-4: These returns demonstrate the benefits of a value indexing methodology. Source: Research Affiliates.

The Fama-French Three-Factor Model

In the early 1990s, Eugene Fama and Kenneth French, both professors at the University of Chicago Booth School of Business, pioneered factor-based index funds when they uncovered a few persistent anomalies that contradicted Fama's earlier work. The so-called "efficient market hypothesis," which Fama had heartily supported, says there are no consistent ways to outperform the market. Yet, to their own surprise, these two academics found that by algorithmically selecting stocks with smaller market capitalizations and lower price-to-book ratios, they could consistently outperform the market. (The third factor, market risk, is not considered a fundamental factor.) Thus, market capitalization and price-to-book ratios became the first inputs used to create factor-based indexes, which in time gave rise to fundamental indexing. Since then, additional factors have been discovered and used to create fundamental-weighted index funds.

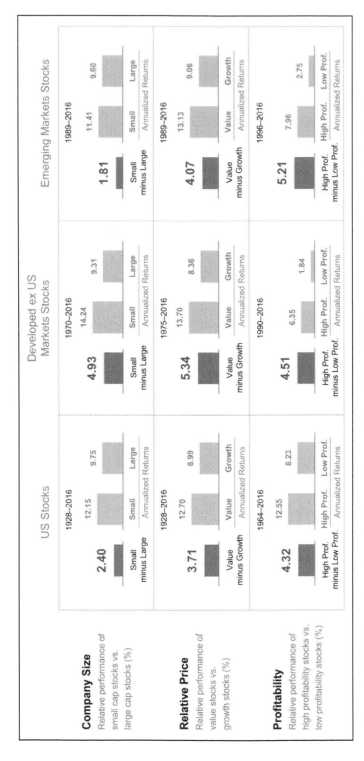

Figure 9-6: This figure shows how the factors Fama and French identified have corresponded to historical outperformance from 1926-2016. Source: Dimensional Fund Advisors.

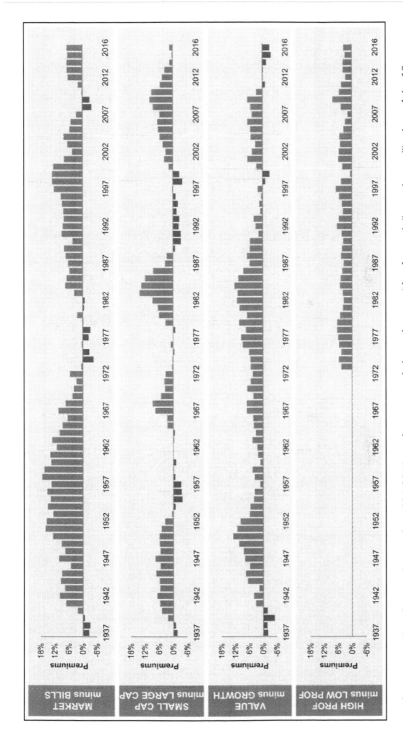

Figure 9-7: This figure shows the 1926-2016 performance of these factors (the factors' "premiums") viewed in 10-year increments. Source: Dimensional Fund Advisors.

Isn't This Just Stock-Picking All Over Again?

Some might argue that these different variations on indexing, such as choosing a small-cap index or a value-weighted index, is the same as stock-picking, which, as we know, is a loser's game. But it really is possible to increase expected returns by using these strategies *so long as we stay within the bounds of indexing*.

> "While much has changed over the years, some things remain the same. There is still a strong relation between risk and expected return, and price-scaled fundamental variables (such as book-to-market) still have explanatory power for stocks returns. Some things have stood the test of time."
>
> – James L. Davis, Author
> *Digging the Panama Canal*

To understand how this is different, we need to understand the difference between the unique risk posed by stock-picking and the risks inherent in real economic activity. The first type of risk is something we should avoid because it comes with no real benefits. Either we will find out that we aren't as good as we think we are when it comes to stock-picking, or we will actually be pretty good, but still not good enough to make up for all the fees and higher taxes. We do, however, want exposure to the latter kind of risk (the risks inherent in real economic activity) because this is the kind of risk that must be undertaken in order for any real economic value to ever be created and in the long run it has rewarded patient investors handsomely.

With stock-picking, we are in effect saying, "I think I'm smarter than everyone else, so I'll take the risk that I'm wrong. I can spot a mispricing and have superior knowledge of the fair price of these stocks compared to the entire marketplace and the pricing mechanism." But by taking on real economic risk by investing in index funds, we are saying instead, "I know I can't possibly be smarter than everyone else on every aspect of the economy, and stock picking is super hard even for the people who get paid full-time to do it. But I will, however, allow myself to bear some of the risks that corporate managers and companies take within their own areas of expertise whenever they try doing something new to improve the value they add to the world."

A good example of this is when Sam Walton (founder of Walmart) became the first discount retailer to purchase a dedicated satellite communications system so that his stores could share their best merchandizing insights more easily. Walton was taking a big risk. His purchase of the satellite equipment could turn out to be a complete waste of money. But he took that risk because, as an expert in merchandizing, he knew what a breakthrough it would be to have the greatest insights from each store shared immediately to all the other stores. Since merchandizing was his specialty, he could see more clearly the pot of gold at the end of the rainbow, and so he believed the risk was worth it. But this is not something an individual investor could have known by parsing through all the data on Walmart. Instead, by owning Walmart stock (and ideally in an index fund) investors were showing a willingness to bear the risk that Sam Walton would be wrong sometimes, but that because of his specialization and ability, when he would be right it would be in a major way. As it turns out, the investment in the satellite communications equipment was a major success.

When we use non-traditional index funds, we are not saying "this stock will do better than that one" or "this CEO is better than that CEO." That would be taking on the stock-picker's risk. Instead, we are over-weighting towards the factors that have historically provided higher expected returns, backed by empirical data, to say things like "Small-cap stocks *tend* to grow faster than large-cap stocks because they have more room for growth," or "Stocks with good value fundamentals *tend to, on average,* outperform the market as a whole." For the value-weighting, it is favoring companies with lots of assets and earnings to work with compared to their size, over companies with small amounts of assets and earnings to work with when compared to their sizes. It's easy to see how one will be more likely, on average, to do better than the other. And with the diversification that comes from index investing, we can feel confident that we will eventually end up seeing these differences in the results.

> Growth stocks tend to be priced for perfection—whereas value stocks are priced expecting mediocrity. Value stocks have second-class status thrust upon them by the market.

The Big Picture

We will close out this chapter by focusing in on the major, overarching benefits that come from the non-traditional index funds we have covered. Equal-, small-cap-, and value-weighted indexes all, in one way or another, force managers to follow the discipline of buying low and selling high—the most fundamental rule of all investing.

- **Equal-Weighted Indexes** force their managers to sell the most popular stocks as their prices climb their peaks, and use the proceeds to buy more stock of the companies whose stock prices have lagged behind.

- **Small-Cap Weighted Indexes** force their managers to sell stocks when their prices rise enough to push them out of the "small-cap" category, and use the proceeds to buy stocks whose prices have fallen enough to put them back in the "small-cap" category or buy newcomers to the index.

- **Value-Weighted Indexes** force their managers to sell stocks whose prices have outpaced their earnings growth (or some other fundamental measure), and use those proceeds to buy stocks whose prices have not kept pace with their earnings growth.

Of course, there are real and meaningful differences between these three types of index funds, but our basic point is that they all have a *constructive* bias towards following the most basic and fundamental rule of investing—and they do it automatically, and without any overpaid managers.

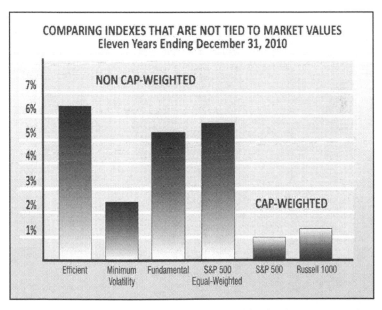

Figure 9-8: Cap-weighted indexes were held back when compared to their non-traditional counterparts over the most recent decade for the reasons discussed in this chapter. Source: Journal of Indexes.

We can see this in Figure 9-8, where it shows that equal-weighted indexes, fundamental-weighted indexes, and even an index weighted to minimize volatility all outperformed cap-weighted indexes over the eleven-year period ending December 31, 2010.

The Next Step: Strategy Models?

In addition to index funds based on factor models, index funds are now being offered that focus on companies implementing specific strategies for rewarding shareholders. For example, there are now index funds that hold only companies with high dividend and buy-back ratios. The figure above shows the "S&P 500 Buyback Index" compared to the regular the S&P 500 index. The buyback index consists of the 100 companies with the highest ratio of cash spent on buybacks versus total market cap.

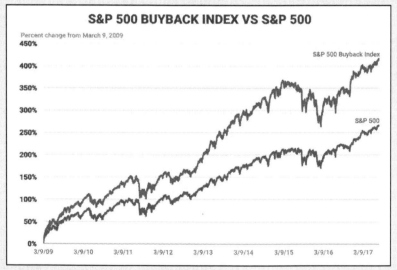

Figure 9-9: The S&P 500 Buyback Index vs the S&P 500®. Source: Business Insider, Bloomberg.

Chapter 10

Exchange-Traded Funds: Moving from Better to Best

> "I love index funds and ETFs. Index funds and ETFs are inexpensive to buy and own. They afford you immediate diversification, and they're extremely tax-efficient investments . . . and you aren't paying exorbitant fees to a fund manager."
>
> – Ben Stein,
> Economist and Humorist

When we debate the pros and cons of investing in an S&P 500® *mutual fund* versus an S&P 500® *exchange traded fund* we are talking about two different ways of implementing the same basic approach. In this case, the underlying approach is that of holding an investment portfolio designed to mimic the S&P 500® Index. What we are debating, then, is not the underlying approach but which of the different investment vehicles we should use.

What Are ETFs?

ETFs are a relatively new creation. They are similar to mutual funds in that they represent a portfolio of stocks selected either by the decisions of an active manager or the passive algorithms of an index fund approach. However, unlike mutual funds, the shares of ETFs also trade on stock exchanges as though they were stocks themselves.

Mutual funds have been around longer than ETFs and trade

through a complex network of middlemen who connect the dots necessary to execute a trade. This makes it more difficult and costly to get in and out of mutual funds than it is for exchange-traded stocks. By trading on exchanges, just like stocks, ETFs essentially replace the middlemen in mutual fund trading with the automated dot-connecting technology of a modern stock exchange. This allows ETFs to cut their costs even further. The increase in trading efficiency also makes the shares of ETFs more "liquid", which means the gaps between bid and ask prices are usually narrower, costing investors still less to get in and out of these funds. To put it bluntly, ETFs are—all else equal—the most cost-efficient, tax-efficient, and liquid vehicles for index-based investing ever created.

> **Think of ETFs as mutual funds on steroids.**

The vast majority of ETFs are passive index funds, designed to contain a predefined and objectively weighted group of securities. However, there are also some actively managed ETFs available, and so we can't just assume that any ETF will be a low-cost index ETF. Nevertheless, with the great majority of ETFs being passive index funds, it's fair to say that most ETFs follow a rules-based, algorithmic approach when it comes to making investment decisions. While the primary benefit of this approach is that it allows the costs to be low, it has the added benefit of preventing "style drift." Style drift is where an actively managed fund deviates from its stated investment strategy. Whatever the reason, the result is the same—investors often end up holding an investment that isn't what they think it is.

Style Drift

Style drift is when a fund manager deviates from his or her stated investment style over time. Sometimes this is due to a change in the investment climate that properly needs to be addressed—in which case the manager should change the stated investment style he or she advertises and communicate this change to his or her investors. Often, however, style drift results from attempts to chase investment returns and/or make up for past underperformance.

For these and other reasons, ETFs have been an extraordinary success story for financial innovation, having gone from almost nothing in 2003 to nearly $3.0 trillion in assets under management in 2017. Today, there are over 2,000 ETFs available for trading on U.S. exchanges. We can see this incredible growth in Figure 10-1.

Simply Superior

In the October 2011 issue of *Investing/Fund Watch*, writer Stan Luxenberg could already see the writing on the wall:

> "ETFs are likely to continue their assault on the traditional turf of mutual funds. During the past decade, ETFs have grown steadily. ETF assets totaled $1.1 trillion in July [2011], up 23 percent from the year before . . . Much of the growth can be traced to advisors who have been enthusiastic users of ETFs . . . *Of RIAs who oversee $250 million to $1 billion in assets, 99 percent use ETFs.*" (emphasis added)

This trend has continued from 2011 to the present, which should not be surprising, given the advantages of ETFs. Also note that RIAs are large users of ETFs, which makes sense given the relatively high fiduciary standard they are held to (see Chapter 3).

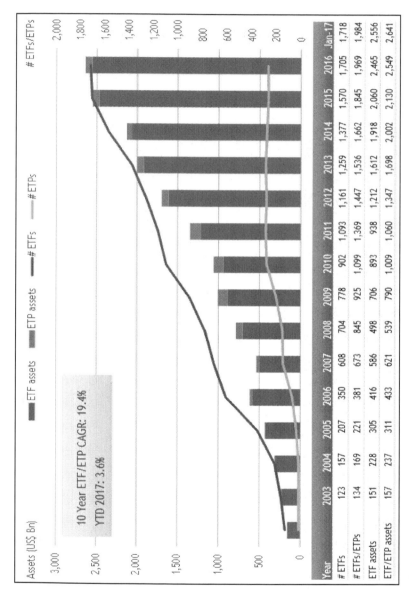

Year	2003	2004	2005	2006	2007	2008	2009	2010	2011	2012	2013	2014	2015	2016	Jan-17
# ETFs	123	157	207	350	608	704	778	902	1,093	1,161	1,259	1,377	1,570	1,705	1,718
# ETFs/ETPs	134	169	221	381	673	845	925	1,099	1,369	1,447	1,536	1,662	1,845	1,969	1,984
ETF assets	151	228	305	416	586	498	706	893	938	1,212	1,612	1,918	2,060	2,465	2,556
ETF/ETP assets	157	237	311	433	621	539	790	1,009	1,060	1,347	1,698	2,002	2,130	2,549	2,641

Figure 10-1: ETFs have grown with incredible speed over the past two decades. For our purposes, we can ignore the tiny amount of ETPs (exchange-traded products), which include things like exchange traded bonds and other non-equity, non-index investments. Source: EFTGI.

Funds Unleashed

It's easy for us to just say "ETFs trade like stocks." But there's a risk that if we just stopped there, readers might not pick up on all the implications. So, we'll take a moment to spell them out here. Since "ETFs trade like stocks":

- They don't require any special accounts and incur no rollover costs.

- They trade continuously throughout the day, allowing investors to buy and sell ETF shares at efficient prices during the day. Mutual funds typically trade only at the market's closing price (known as "forward pricing").

- They can be bought and sold on margin.

- They can be sold short.

- They are optionable, meaning speculators can wager on future price movements without purchasing the ETFs directly.

- They can be an attractive alternative to derivatives and futures contracts for hedging against market risks, since they can be sold short, in smaller sizes, and more cheaply. In some cases, where simply aren't futures or derivatives contracts for hedging, ETFs may be the only option.

This last point, about using ETFs for hedging, is of little use to most investors, but there's an indirect benefit all investors receive by virtue of this practice by others. The use of ETFs in hedging means ETFs are traded more frequently by large players in the stock market. This makes the market for ETFs even more liquid, which again lowers costs and makes it even easier to trade.

This raises the question, "What benefits do ETFs have to offer the average investor in particular?" As we've already hinted, for investors who want to follow the approach outlined in this book, ETFs are an ideal investment vehicle because of how they allow investors to implement the kind of indexing strategy covered in Chapters 7-9, achieve the kind of diversification discussed in Chapter 6, and avoid the pitfalls discussed in Chapters 2-5, *all while achieving these goals at even lower costs, greater tax efficiency, and greater flexibility*. We will now cover each of these specific benefits to investors in more detail.

Lower Costs

ETFs have many advantages over mutual funds when it comes to cutting costs. They can receive shares from large investors, like pension funds, which allows them to lower the cost of acquiring the shares. Operating expenses are also lower because ETFs, unlike mutual funds, are not required to maintain individual records on each shareholder. Instead, the brokerage firms for those holding the ETFs bear this responsibility, which they can do more cheaply because they already have all their clients' information. ETFs also need minimal cash on hand for redemptions (which holds back returns for mutual funds) because instead of shareholders buying and selling their shares directly from the fund (as in the case with mutual funds) they buy and sell their shares from each other in market exchanges. ETFs also, in general, incur fewer costs from various regulatory, reporting, and recordkeeping requirements.

This is why, as we saw in Figure 10-1, the popularity of ETFs is rising quickly, and as they rise they are rapidly replacing mutual funds. This growth has led to even more cost-cutting benefits for investors. As ETFs have grown, so too has competition among the firms that run ETFs and the brokers who help investors trade in ETFs. As a result of this ongoing price war (see sidebar, "The Race to The Bottom"), many ETFs in the major investment categories carry fees under 0.10% with some as low as 0.03%. And many major brokerage firms now charge zero commissions on some ETF purchases. This means that a diversified portfolio of exchange traded funds can be established with management fees 90% lower than the typical actively managed fund.

The Race to The Bottom

The *Wall Street Journal* reported on Jan. 26, 2016:

> In November, asset manager BlackRock Inc. said it would slash by more than 50% the annual expenses charged to investors in an exchange-traded fund that aims to mimic the performance of the entire U.S. stock market.

> By the end of the day, executives at rival Charles Schwab Corp. had matched the price cut. In December, Vanguard Group announced fee cuts of as much as 25% at dozens of its funds.

> The cost of investing is tumbling toward zero for some basic portfolios of stocks and bonds as firms duel for customers.

"Fees on Mutual Funds and ETFs Tumble Toward Zero", *Wall Street Journal*, Jan. 26, 2016.

Tax Efficiency

ETFs offer greater tax efficiency by eliminating the sometimes-sizable phantom income taxes that can be created by mutual funds. An investor who purchases mutual fund shares in late-December may receive a 1099 IRS Form for the net realized taxable gains on that investment made at any time during the year, even if he didn't earn a penny or make a trade after the initial purchase. ETFs, on the other hand, typically pass virtually no phantom income tax through to the investor. These and other advantages make ETFs ideal for long-term investing.

> ETFs enable the investor to compound portfolio growth with minimal current tax consequence, even when profitable trades are made within the fund itself.

ETFs can also exchange shares with very large shareholders looking to close their ETF positions. While this lowers the trading costs only slightly, it is a more significant benefit when it comes to tax-efficiency. By avoiding the actual purchase and sale of shares through these shares-for-shares exchanges, ETFs are able to avoid incurring capital gains taxes within the fund itself, meaning more of the returns can be kept for investors. These small savings in costs and substantial reductions in tax liabilities often add up to large gains in the long-run. These advantages further tip the balance in favor of ETFs over mutual funds.

Flexibility

Another advantage of ETFs is the flexibility they provide when it comes to customizing a portfolio. As WisdomTree Director of Institutional Sales and Trading, David J. Abner explains in his book *The ETF Handbook: How to Value and Trade Exchange Traded Funds*:

> "In the same way that Lego building blocks are used by both children and adults to make creations of all sizes,

ETFs are the portfolio building blocks of the modern age, usable by investors of all sizes and for a variety of portfolio demands." (page xvii)

ETFs work well as building blocks for a variety of reasons. For one, the lower transaction costs and their ability to be traded midday makes it easier and less expensive to swap out one of these "blocks" for another. Another reason is that ETFs often follow stripped-down, bare-bones investment strategies as a way to keep their costs low, which has the effect of creating "blocks" with more clearly defined edges. In some cases, ETFs are even created with this kind of building-block role in mind, since this is an approach that lines up well with the ideas of modern finance and it is something increasingly desired by large institutional investors who want to put these building-block approaches to use.

With so many advantages to ETFs, it may be a wonder that some people use mutual funds at all to implement an indexing approach to investing. One reason, perhaps, is that mutual fund shareholders can often buy or sell shares of index mutual funds at no cost, whereas buying ETF shares typically does require paying a commission to a broker. But when using a discount broker, these costs can be as little as $5 or $10 per purchase, which would represent a 0.1% or less commission on a $10,000 investment. For the long-term investor, these costs are immaterial and are a small, one-time price to pay for avoiding the higher management fees of mutual funds that would reduce your returns every year, continuously. In fact, as we noted earlier, even the commissions on ETF trades are becoming less and less of an issue as more and more brokerage firms are allowing customers to buy some ETFs for no commission at all.

ETFs Compared with Index Mutual Funds and Other Mutual Funds

	ETFs	Index Mutual Funds	Mutual Funds (actively managed)
Ownership	↑ Bought on a stock exchange	↑ Purchased directly from the fund	↑ Purchased directly from the fund
Management Style	↑ Either passively or actively managed	↑ Passively managed	↑ Actively managed
Pricing	↑ Traded throughout the trading day ↑ Limit orders, short selling, margin buying and options trading available	↑ NAV once per day after market close ↑ May require a minimum initial investment	↑ NAV once per day after market close ↑ May require a minimum initial investment
Cost	↑ Ongoing management fees ↑ Brokerage and trading costs	↑ Ongoing management fees ↑ Possible sales charges and redemption fees	↑ Ongoing management fees ↑ Possible sales charges and redemption fees
Transparency	↑ Underlying holdings disclosed daily	↑ Holdings generally disclosed monthly or quarterly	↑ Holdings generally disclosed monthly or quarterly
Taxes	↑ Typically extremely tax-efficient with dividends flowing through to shareholders (if any) and minimal additional taxable income	↑ Can be extremely tax-inefficient. Frequently phantom taxable income can be generated even when there is no real economic gain to the shareholder	↑ Can be extremely tax-inefficient. Frequently phantom taxable income can be generated even when there is no real economic gain to the shareholder

Figure 10-2: This figure is a summary of the key differences between index mutual funds and mutual funds in general. Source: RVW Research.

Chapter 11

The Role of Bonds in a Portfolio

> "I would never do 100% of anything."
>
> – John C. Bogle

Despite the superiority of stocks in many respects, bonds still have a proper role to play in an investment portfolio. As we've covered exhaustively, stocks shine in the long run—but go through painful bear markets along the way. Bonds, on the other hand, are just the opposite: they tend to fare well in the short-run (even during bear markets) and poorly in the long-run (relative to stocks). In this way stocks and bonds complement each other, with stocks serving as the tool to meet long-term investment goals and bonds serving as the tool to prepare for meeting short-term needs and obligations. As a bonus, including bonds in a portfolio lowers the overall volatility of the portfolio and provides a more predictable stream of income.

What Exactly is a Bond?

A bond is a contract (as in "Your word is your *bond*") between a company and the bondholder. The bondholder lends money upfront to the company (or buys it from another bondholder) in exchange for a legally-binding promise from the company to pay interest and principal to the bondholder on the specified dates. This differs from a stock, where dividends can change (or even be discontinued), and there are no protections in place to secure the original invested amount (the principal). While there are no guarantees in investing (even insurance companies can fail), the initial investment in a bond is much more likely to be repaid or recovered than the initial investment in a stock. This is because, legally, bondholders get to stand in line ahead of the stockholders when a company goes bankrupt. Before the stockholders can get a dime, all of the bondholder need to be repaid in full. This is part of what makes stocks riskier—the entire value of the company could be wiped out while repaying the bondholders before the line ever makes it to the stockholders.

The Domesticated Bond

Think of bonds as the domesticated cousins of stocks—less imbued with raw natural power, but easier to control. There is a greater sense of control with bonds because they impose more rigid conditions on the underlying companies and extract more clearly defined promises.

And like domesticated dog breeds, bonds come in all kinds of shapes and sizes: taxable, tax-free, Treasury, investment-grade, high-yield, and more. And, perhaps surprisingly, they come in such a variety for the same reason: Mankind has carefully refined and tailored their characteristics through the ages to satisfy a variety of different needs and interests.

If we circle back to stocks for a moment, this issue of where stockholders and bondholders stand in line (referred to as "capital structure") can help us better understand why stocks *must* provide a better return in the long-run compared to bonds. As explained by investment manager Rob Arnott:

"Stocks ought to produce higher returns than bonds in order for the capital markets to 'work.' Otherwise, stockholders would not be paid for the additional risk they take for being lower down the capital structure. It comes as no surprise, therefore, that stockholders have enjoyed outsized returns for their efforts."

How Bonds Enhance *Life* Stability

Despite the relatively low returns for bonds, the priority given to bondholders makes bonds a better investment vehicle when it comes to ensuring that you will have access to cash when you need it in a week, a month, or a year. An investor with an all-stock portfolio may find himself in need of money in the midst of a bear market and forced to sell investments at a fraction of the initial price—also missing out on the gains that would eventually follow when the longer-term uptrend in equities resumes.

By creating a bond portfolio (within an overall investment portfolio), investors can schedule the timing for when they want to access these funds according to their own life plans and goals. (This will be explained in more detail later in the chapter.) However—and this is the important part—even if your life doesn't go as planned and you have to sell some bonds early (i.e. a few months before their maturity dates), it's not as bad as being forced to sell stocks during a downturn. This is because bond prices are less volatile, and they become even less volatile as they approach their maturity dates, meaning the price is unlikely to be much lower than what you'd get by waiting all the way to the maturity date. This characteristic of how quickly an asset can be converted to cash without much loss is what is meant by "liquidity."

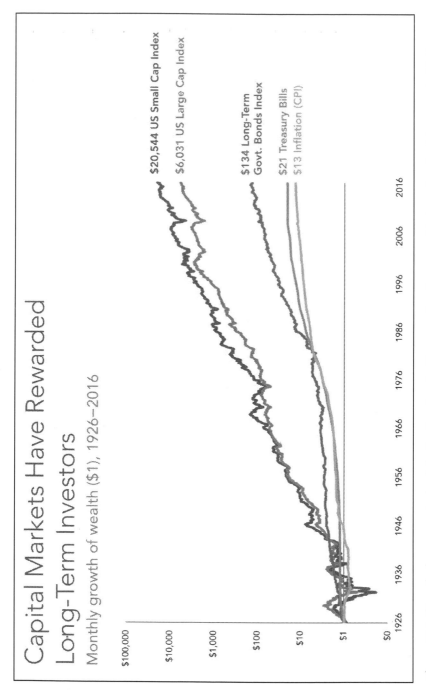

Figure 11-1: Over the long-run, stocks do better than bonds. However, bonds are good to have for short-term needs. Notice how bonds fared much better at the start of The Great Depression (bottom left). Source: Dimensional Fund Advisors.

How Bonds Enhance *Portfolio* Stability

Short-term cash needs are about having stability in day-to-day life. Portfolio stability is about having stability on the screen (or in an account statement). This is an important, but often overlooked, objective. As part of a portfolio, bonds act as a buffer against the volatility of stocks, while stocks dampen the volatility of bonds. This synergy increases the consistency of total portfolio returns. Statistically, holding a combination of stocks and bonds has the potential to generate returns close to those seen in a stock-only investment strategy while, at the same time, substantially lowering the risk of being fully invested in stocks alone.

Tax Benefits

In addition to the stability benefits covered so far, high-income investors can use certain tax-free* bonds as a way to provide tax-free income. Payments from most municipal bonds are exempt from federal income taxes and often state income taxes as well. Municipal bonds are issued by state, city, and local governments to pay for infrastructure and general expenses. These bonds are often called "munis" for short. Because of their tax advantages, they need to offer less of an incentive for investors, and so they often pay lower interest rates than corporate bonds. Nevertheless, in the full analysis, they can often be highly competitive investments.

Taxable vs. Tax-free Bonds

The lower interest rates tax-free bonds pay balances out against the aggregate tax benefits for all of the investors in the bonds. But while all bondholders get paid the same interest rate, they do not all share the same tax benefits due to their different tax brackets. This

---

* Throughout this chapter, when we say "tax-free," we mean bonds that are free of federal (and sometimes state) *income* taxes. There may still be non-income taxes that apply. This, however, shouldn't change the general points being made.

makes tax-free bonds a winning deal for those in the higher tax-brackets and a losing deal for those in the lower tax-brackets who are unwittingly subsidizing those in the higher tax-brackets by accepting a tax benefit that's not big enough to make up for the lower interest rate payments they are getting.

The only way to figure out where you stand in this balance is to do an "apples-to-apples" comparison between taxable and tax-free bonds from the perspective of your own tax situation. To do this, you first need to calculate the "equivalent taxable interest rate" for the tax-free bonds you are considering. The "equivalent taxable interest rate" tells us the interest rate we would need to get from a taxable bond in order to make it just as attractive as the tax-free bonds. If the rate is better than we can get from taxable bonds, then tax-free bonds are a good choice. If we can find taxable bonds that pay an even higher rate, then they are the way to go.

Dividend-Payers as a Bond Alternative

For investors interested in bonds for income purposes, it may be worth considering dividend-paying stocks. As the chart below shows, these have not only outperformed bonds, but also stocks, while having the benefit of producing dividend income. **In addition, most dividends are taxed more favorably than interest income.**

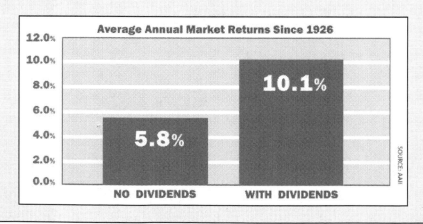

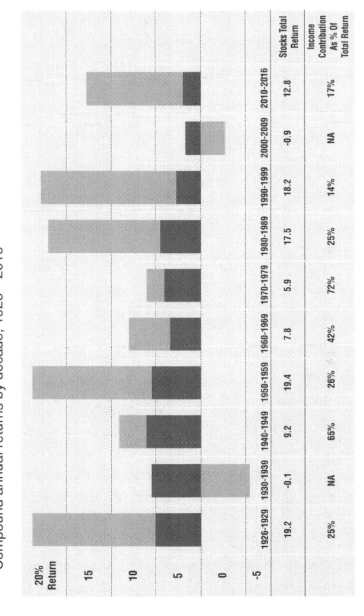

Contribution of Dividends to Total Market Returns
Compound annual returns by decade, 1926–2016

	1926-1929	1930-1939	1940-1949	1950-1959	1960-1969	1970-1979	1980-1989	1990-1999	2000-2009	2010-2016
Stocks Total Return	19.2	-0.1	9.2	19.4	7.8	5.9	17.5	18.2	-0.9	12.8
Income Contribution As % Of Total Return	25%	NA	65%	26%	42%	72%	25%	14%	NA	17%

■ Price Return   ■ Dividend Income

Figure 11-2: When talking about income needs for investors, we shouldn't forget about the substantial role dividends play in generating the total returns we see for equities. Source: RVW Research.

Determining the equivalent taxable interest rate for a tax-free bond starts with knowing your own marginal income tax rate, including federal, state, and local income taxes. If you are in the 28% federal bracket, with state taxes of 9%, and local taxes of 3%, your marginal tax rate is around 37%.* That rate is used in the following formula:

$$Equivalent\ Taxable\ Interest\ Rate = \frac{100 \times taxfree\ interest\ rate}{100 - marginal\ tax\ rate}$$

So, if you were evaluating a municipal bond with a 4% coupon, the formula would tell us that an equivalent taxable yield is about 6.35%:

$$Equivalent\ Taxable\ Interest\ Rate = \frac{100 \times 0.04}{100 - 0.37} = 6.35\%$$

Thus, if we can find a taxable bond with a yield of more than 6.35%, coupled with the degree of safety we are seeking, the taxable bond would provide more after-tax income than the 4% tax-free municipal bond and would be the better choice.

Most individuals in the higher income tax brackets will benefit by owning tax-free bonds. However, no matter how high the tax bracket, it is almost never appropriate to hold tax-free bonds in a qualified retirement account (e.g., Keogh, SEP, 401(k), 403(b), IRA/ Roth IRA) because the otherwise tax-free interest payments received will be taxed upon withdrawal, defeating the tax-free advantage and resulting in a loss of potential income.

---

* Combined marginal tax rates depend on the deductibility of state and local taxes on individual investors' federal tax returns, and miscellaneous deductions.

A Warning on Munis and AMT

The issue of taxes is rarely straightforward, and the Alternative Minimum Tax (AMT) often impacts unwary municipal bond holders. The AMT may cause the interest from certain municipal bonds—especially those used to fund airports and industrial projects—to be counted as income for some taxpayers, negating the value of otherwise tax-free bonds. Understanding the specifics of how the AMT may or may not affect the bonds you are considering is beyond the scope of this book and usually requires the assistance of both your accountant and investment advisor.

When purchasing individual bonds, it is possible to avoid the types of munis that can trigger these AMT considerations. However, mutual funds and ETFs that invest in municipal bonds might hold these types of AMT-triggering municipal bonds, which means they will regularly distribute income subject to the AMT to their shareholders. Although municipal bonds with an exposure to AMT frequently offer slightly higher interest rates than other munis, it is rarely enough to offset the actual tax liability.

Bond Risks

No investment is without risk. And while bonds are thought of as a safe investment, there are still some important risk factors to be aware of. During the period of time between when you buy and when you sell a bond or redeem it at the maturity date, its price can and will fluctuate. It is only when the bondholder holds the bond all the way to the maturity date that he or she gets to cash in on the legal agreement to get paid in full. In the meantime, the prices will go up and down based on a variety of factors, including but not limited to interest rate risks, credit risks, default risks, inflation risks, reinvestment risks, and time risks.

Interest Rate Risks

Interest rates change frequently, and these changes are too difficult to predict. Bond prices are inversely related to changes in interest rates; when rates increase, the prices of the bonds you are holding will decrease, and vice versa. The interest rate on a bond is defined at the time the bond is first offered for sale. This interest rate, known as the *coupon*, will be based on interest rates in the general economy at the time the bond is issued. Over time, market rates change, but the coupon does not. If interest rates move higher, investors may not be willing to buy the bonds at face (or par) value. For example, if an investor buys a bond with a 4% coupon and interest rates rise to 5%, new issues will have to pay 5% and no one would be likely to buy a 4% bond at its par value.

To help ensure there is someone willing to buy the bond, the market revalues the price of the 4% bond lower ("at a discount" from $1,000) so that the eventual repayment of principal, together with the interest payments over time, will offset the lower coupon rate. This should not matter to an investor holding the bond to maturity, since the principal will be repaid in full at that time (unless you also purchased the bond at a "premium,"—an amount greater than $1,000—in which case the "yield to maturity" will be even lower).

Default Risks

Occasionally, companies go out of business or file for bankruptcy. This poses a risk for both stock- and bondholders for all of their holdings. If this happens, the value of a company's stock will fall to zero and the value of a company's bonds will typically fall below the amount initially invested. Only US Treasury bonds are completely free of this "default risk" because the government has the ability to print more money as a last resort to make its payments.

Inflation Risks

Another factor that influences bond interest rates is the prospect of inflation. Inflation eats away at the purchasing power of your periodic interest payments and also means the principal will be worth less when it is eventually repaid. If there are concerns about future inflation, bond interest rates will usually be higher to compensate investors for this increased risk and to attract their money.

> Inflation favors the borrower and robs the lender. Over time, both the principal and the interest will provide shrinking buying power to the bond investor.

Reinvestment Risk

Bonds also have a unique risk factor known as *reinvestment risk*. Just as it is impossible to predict the stock market, it is impossible to reliably predict the general interest rates in the economy. In the early 1980s, long-term U.S. Treasury bonds offered double digit yields because inflation had been running rampant for nearly a decade. By the time these bonds were fully repaid, inflation was under control (almost non-existent through most of the 1990s and 2000s) and there were no new low-risk alternatives available to investors offering this high level of income. Reinvestment risk means an investor may suffer a real drop in current income if he or she is unable to lock-in the same interest rate in the future economic environment.

Bond Volatility for Different Maturities

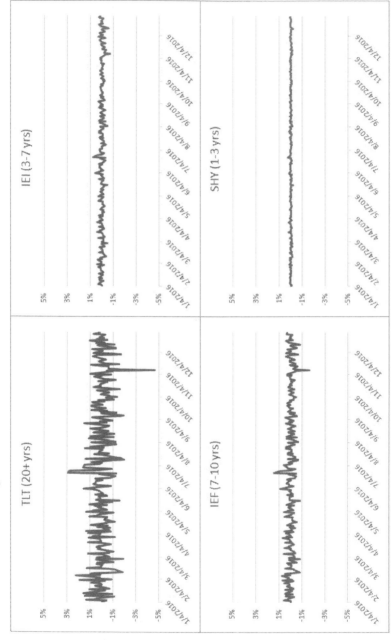

Figure 11-3: This figure shows the daily percent price changes for four different ETFs that follow bonds of different maturities. Volatility is greatest for bonds with the longest maturities (20+ years) and diminishes to an almost imperceptible level for shorter term bonds (1-3 years).

Bond Volatility

It is widely believed that bonds are less volatile than stocks. While this is generally true if you plan to hold a bond to maturity (the day when the principal is scheduled to be repaid), it is not always true when investors hold bonds for shorter periods and sell before the maturity date. Impatient trading in bond markets can even lead to rare situations where bonds experience greater volatility than stocks. Over the long term, government bonds tend to have half as much volatility as stocks. However, the annualized standard deviation of bonds is about 10%, which means you can lose a significant amount of money in any given year.

Bond Ladders

For affluent investors, it often makes sense to hold bonds directly through individual bonds instead of holding them indirectly through bond funds.* This approach allows an investor to create a customized schedule of bond maturity dates, commonly known as a "bond ladder." And while this requires more thought and effort than choosing a bond fund, the benefits are well worth it. Alternatively, there are now target date bond ETFs that are designed to end at fixed future dates. These are ideal for constructing a bond ladder with smaller portfolios.

How Bond Ladders Work

Bond ladders take the risk-reducing benefits of bonds and go a step further by optimizing the holdings within that category. The goal of a bond ladder is to take advantage of the greater stability provided by shorter-term bonds while at the same time benefitting from the higher returns provided by longer-term bonds.

---

* This is because affluent investors can afford to buy bonds in large enough chunks to spread out the associated fees and make them comparable to those of a bond funds on a percentage basis.

If we were to build a bond portfolio where all of the bonds in the portfolio were short-term bonds set to mature on the same date, while we would have a great deal of funds at our disposal (liquidity) in case of an emergency, we would also get a much lower interest rate, meaning we would need to set aside an even greater sum of money for bonds and less for our long-term breadwinner, stocks. And further, we would be exposing ourselves even more frequently to the reinvestment risks we covered in the "Reinvestment Risks" section above. After each brief time period, when the bonds would mature, we would be forced to reinvest all the eggs in our bond basket at the same prevailing interest rate — whatever that might be. And, again and again, we would have to do this many times more than we would with longer-term bonds.

Conversely, if in our bond portfolio we held only long-term bonds with the same maturity date — thinking we could sell them off piecemeal to meet our needs as they arise — we would run into a different, but similar, problem. Since the prices of longer-term bonds are more strongly influenced by the daily changes in market interest rates (see Figure 11-2), we could find ourselves in a situation somewhat similar to the trap we run into with stocks. There could be something like a periodic, but major downturn in the value of long-term bonds, and if we were forced to sell some off piecemeal to meet our needs or deal with an emergency, we might find that we are forced to sell these bonds at a significantly reduced price than where we bought them. And, here, too, we would still be exposing ourselves to a higher reinvestment risk by having the bonds all mature on the same date. If interest rates were low at that time, we'd have no choice but to accept them for our entire bond portfolio.

Laddering solves these problems by using a mixture of short-term and longer-term bonds with maturity dates spread out across time. For example, to construct a five-year bond ladder, we would invest equal amounts of money in bonds maturing one, two, three, four, and five years from now. After the first year passes (when the 1-year bonds are due) we would reinvest the principal in a new 5-year bond. This would effectively move this principal amount to the back of the line. The original two-, three-, four-, and five-year bonds would now be one-, two-, three-, and four-year bonds respectively, since they would all be one year closer to maturity. In the end, we would come right back to the same time-to-maturity structure we started with.

Continuing with our example, this five-year bond ladder would have an average investment period of 2.5 years. However, each time we reinvest, we would be reinvesting in 5-year bonds, which at any given point in time will usually pay a higher interest rate than what you would get from buying 2.5-year bonds, or any other bonds with maturities shorter than five years. And since only one-fifth of the portfolio is being reinvested at the end of each year, we would only be exposing one-fifth of our portfolio to reinvestment risk each year. In this way, the overall reinvestment risk would be lower than both the 100% short-term and 100% long-term bond portfolios.

This would allow us to consistently reinvest all the way through an interest rate cycle: If interest rates fall and you're forced to reinvest at lower rates, you would continue to benefit from the four-fifths of your bond ladder that have locked-in above-market interest rates. And as interest rates rise again, since you will not have fired all your bullets at once, you will be continuing to reinvest each year at the higher rates. In the end, a five-year bond ladder, like the one in this example, will provide a return close to the return of long-term bonds, but with a much lower risk that you will be forced to sell your bonds at a time when you'll get less than you were planning on or that you'll be saddled with low interest rates throughout your bond portfolio.

According to the data shown in Table 11-1, over more than a century, five-year bond ladders have never had a losing year. Since 1900, this strategy has delivered an average return of 4.6% per year, only slightly less than that of bond ladders with longer durations. The consistency of returns for the five-year ladder makes this an ideal strategy for many investors.

	5-year	10-year	20-year
Maximum	15.5%	16.2%	21%
Minimum	0.4%	0.2%	-2.1%
Average	4.6%	4.8%	4.9%

Table 11-1: Five-year bond ladders have provided consistent returns with less volatility compared to longer-term bond ladders. Source: Crestmont Research.

For investors who have both a long time horizon and the psychological ability to handle volatility (i.e. both the emotional and the financial risk tolerance) bonds are usually not needed and a portfolio of 100% equities has historically produced dramatically higher returns in time. The allocation between bonds and equities should always take into account the totality of the investor's assets and expected income flows. An income generating real estate portfolio or a steady income from a trust for example should be viewed as bond alternatives when asset allocation is determined.

BOND BUYERS BEWARE!

While there are many problems that arise when financial advisors sell mutual funds, there are also some things you should know when they sell you bonds:

- *PRICING:* Most brokers sell you bonds at marked-up prices, making an undisclosed profit on the sale. They act not as a broker but as a principal. (Instead you should buy bonds directly from a low-cost provider).

- *TIME HORIZON:* Because bond prices and interest rates move inversely, long-term bonds work well in times of falling interest rates and poorly in times of appreciating rates. At times of relatively low interest rates, long-term bonds offer the likelihood of a severe decline in value as rates rise over time—and the further out you go, the greater this effect. [Suggestion: Use the laddered bond strategy from this chapter, which optimizes returns, stabilizes income and minimizes the losses from holding long-term bonds.]

- *SAFETY:* Buying small issues or unrated ("junk") bonds presents numerous risks, including illiquidity and the loss of principal if the issuer defaults or goes bankrupt (see sidebar "Junk Bonds Offer Little Protection" on page 17).

- *CALLABLE:* Callable bonds are a "heads we win–tails you lose" proposition. If interest rates rise, bond prices will fall and you'll be stuck holding a poorly performing asset at a time when higher yields are available for similar bonds. On the other hand, if rates fall, bond prices will rise, and your bond will probably be "called" (redeemed early) allowing the issuer to refinance at lower rates. You will end up replacing your relatively high interest income with bonds providing a lower return.

- *BOND FUNDS:* Individual bonds have maturity dates, so even if rates move up and values decline, upon maturity the full face amount will ultimately be repaid. Bond funds, on other hand, usually have no maturity date and the loss may never be recovered.

- *ASSET ALLOCATION:* The tendency to seek safety in bonds often misses the point that bonds, too, carry risks. Inflation ultimately impacts both the principal invested and the income.

Chapter 12

Bringing It All Together

> "To invest successfully does not require a stratospheric IQ, unusual business insights, or inside information. What's needed is a sound intellectual framework for making decisions and the ability to keep emotions from corroding the framework."
>
> – Warren Buffett

In Chapters 1 – 5, we covered all the major pitfalls and ways investors set themselves up for failure. Then, in Chapters 6 – 11, we covered all the tools you'll need to set yourself up for investment success. This chapter is where we will tie it together, piecing the insights from all the preceding chapters into the kind of "sound intellectual framework" Buffett refers to in the quote above.

Your Financial Advisor

The first place to start with is your financial advisor. If you don't already have one, then—despite all the bad things we had to say about them in Chapter 3—*we do suggest you get one*. While many financial advisors turn out to be less than virtuous when you look under the hood at how they treat their clients' portfolios, the right advisor—one that is trustworthy and competent—can be an invaluable asset when it comes to handling the emotional impulses covered in Chapter 5. Not only can these impulses (when acted upon) hurt your returns, but when they build up inside you, without having a trusted confidant to talk to, the harm can spread to your mental and even physical health.

A trustworthy and competent advisor can also help you keep perspective and not lose sight of what all is encompassed in planning your financial future. While this book has focused mostly on how to approach constructing an investment portfolio, we also need to be reminded sometimes how balancing our own checkbooks, setting up life insurance, and making sure we have good credit are all matters that we should be attending to. These matters can also have an impact on our financial future and how we can deal with unexpected emergencies. We each also have our own attitudes towards money—feelings shaped by our earliest experiences with it—which may or may not be constructive. These are all aspects of financial planning in its broadest sense where a trustworthy and competent advisor can provide even more help.

Plan B

For those of you with limited means or who are just starting out, superior returns can be reached by purchasing and holding a few index ETFs and rebalancing annually. While you probably won't do as well as someone who can afford a good investment advisor to aide in implementing the more nuanced strategies in this book, you will likely do better than anyone purchasing and holding non-index mutual funds.

You can use this book to help you find a trustworthy and competent investment advisor by using the problems and pitfalls we covered in Chapters 2 and 3 to test the advisor you are considering. Ask questions like, "Is this active mutual fund, after fees and in the long-run, going to outperform an index fund?" Or, "Are mutual fund managers actually good at stock-picking?" Wait for the advisor to give you his or her full response before you say anything further. Later, you can mull over their response and compare it to what's in Chapters 2 and 3. If you feel their responses are, overall, consistent with what's in this book, then you can feel more confident about the advisor under consideration. If, on the other hand, the advisor responds in a way that tries to steer you towards actively managed mutual funds, then you should be suspicious, and—at the very least—you should meet with a good number of other financial advisors before deciding to commit to the one you're considering.

> Past performance is usually overrated—process and character are underrated. Be skeptical when performance is the entire reason for choosing a fund or advisor.

> To illustrate the difference between a good financial advisor and a bad one, consider the following: Holding foreign investments in a retirement accounts means that the benefits of foreign tax credits are lost. Holding them personally gives you a tax credit. *If your advisor made this mistake—which most that we meet do—it's probably time to move on.*

Make a Portfolio Plan

Once you have an investment advisor you can trust, it's time to make an all-encompassing "portfolio plan." At a minimum, this should include: 1) how you will allocate your assets between stocks, bonds, and other asset classes, 2) a written "portfolio *emergency* plan" for responding to market downturns and personal financial emergencies, and 3) a plan for sticking to the plan!

From this point forward, we are going to be taking for granted that you know to invest the stock portion of your portfolio exclusively in low-cost index funds as described in Chapters 6, 7, and 8, and—where possible—to use ETF index funds instead of mutual fund index funds as described in Chapter 10. We will assume going forward that you know to avoid, *no matter what*, any form of stock-picking or market-timing, whether done by you, your advisor, or the manager of a non-index mutual fund. If you have a strong desire to invest in individual stocks, set aside a small sum in a separate account for your stock picking and active trading.

Asset Allocation: Equities vs. Bonds

The first and most basic question to ask when it comes to asset allocation is "What percentage should I put in stocks and what percentage should I put in bonds?"

The simple approach is to follow a rule-of-thumb strategy such as subtracting your age from the number 120 and using the resulting number as your percent allocation to stocks. For example, using this approach, a forty-year-old man would put 80% of his portfolio in stocks (120 – 40 = 80) and the remaining 20% in bonds. For an 80-year-old, the split would be 40/60, with 40% in stocks and 60% in bonds. Of course, no magical formula can tell you exactly what your allocation should be, but when in doubt, this approach is a good place to start. It should give you a very rough approximation in the ballpark of your ideal allocation.

"Investment policy (asset allocation) is the foundation upon which portfolios should be constructed and managed."

– Charles D. Ellis, Former Chairman of the Yale Endowment Committee and the CFA Institute

---

For investors who want a bespoke approach, this is an area where a trustworthy and competent financial advisor can be a great help. Often, they will have you fill out a risk tolerance questionnaire like the sample one on the following pages. A trustworthy and competent advisor will know what types of life circumstances can make it necessary to adjust the basic formulas.

The two key factors that need to be taken into account in determining optimal asset allocation are: 1) Risk tolerance: Your *emotional* ability to withstand portfolio volatility, and 2) Risk ability: Your *financial* ability to do so. In turn, risk ability will be influenced by three factors: 1) current income and projected retirement age, 2) passive income sources (real estate, trust income, social security), and 3) anticipated lifestyle costs annually and in retirement (if applicable).

Leaving Something Behind

For those whose goals include providing for family members (or perhaps a cause or foundation), the simple 120-formula will not suffice. Including these goals effectively extends the investment horizon beyond your own lifetime. Charles Ellis, a former chairman of the Yale Endowment Committee as well as the CFA Institute, explains this well in his book *Timeless Strategies for Successful Investing*:

> If, for example, you plan to leave most of your capital in bequests to your children, the appropriate time horizon for your family investment policy--even if you are well into your seventies or eighties--may well be so long-term that you'd be correct to ignore such investment conventions as the canard, "older people should invest in bonds for higher income and greater safety."

Sample Risk Tolerance Questionnaire

To determine your own level of risk tolerance, it can be very helpful to answer a few questions. These questions are often presented to investors in the form of a questionnaire similar to the one below.

1. The average 65-year-old can expect to live an additional 20 to 25 years. With that in mind, and based on your own health status and family history, do you believe your health is:

    A. Better than average
    B. Average
    C. Below average

2. Sometimes investment losses are permanent, sometimes they are prolonged, and sometimes they are short-lived. With that in mind, if you experienced significant investment losses, would you:

    A. Consider selling immediately any investments that have substantially declined
    B. Continue to follow your long-term investment strategy
    C. Consider buying more of an investment that had substantially declined

3. Which best describes your response to the following statement: I am comfortable with volatile investments that may frequently experience large declines in value if there is a potential for higher returns. Do you:

    A. Strongly disagree
    B. Disagree
    C. Somewhat agree
    D. Agree
    E. Strongly agree

4. Over time, you probably know that inflation can significantly affect the amount of goods and services that you will be able to purchase. However, you may not know that there is a higher degree of risk with a portfolio that has long-term returns that significantly exceed inflation. With that in mind, which of the following choices best reflects your investment approach? Do you want to:

    A. Avoid losses, although your investments might not keep pace with inflation
    B. Keep pace with inflation, while taking on a moderate level of risk
    C. Take on higher levels of risk and tolerate investment losses in attempt to exceed inflation

Sample Risk Tolerance Questionnaire (Continued)

5. Assume that you are receiving income each month from a specific investment in your portfolio. The value of that income changes based on the investment's performance and it currently yields $1,000. If you had a loss, at what point would you consider making a change in the investment?

    A. Your monthly income declines to $970 (a 3% loss)
    B. Your monthly income declines to $940 (a 6% loss)
    C. Your monthly income declines to $900 (a 10% loss)
    D. Your monthly income declines to $820 (an 18% loss)
    E. You would not make changes in the first year

6. Which best describes your response to the following statement: If the U.S. stock portion of my portfolio were to lose 10% of its value over a one-month period, consistent with the overall market, I would prefer to cut my losses and shift into a more conservative investment strategy. Do you:

    A. Strongly agree
    B. Agree
    C. Somewhat agree
    D. Disagree
    E. Strongly disagree

7. Consider what might happen over the next year to the portfolio that provides your income. Which of these income changes are you most comfortable with? (Assume you are meeting your needs and could stand some loss of income, although it might be inconvenient.)

    A. Portfolio A: a likely increase in income of 2% and a slight chance of a lower income
    B. Portfolio B: a likely increase in income of 5% and a moderate chance of a lower income
    C. Portfolio C: a likely increase in income of 8% and a significant chance of a lower income

8. If leaving a bequest would cause you to fall short of your income needs, what would you do?

    A. I do not plan to leave a bequest
    B. Lower the income goal because a bequest is more important
    C. Nothing because a bequest and income are equally important
    D. Reduce the amount set aside for a bequest because income is more important than the size of the bequest

9. What is your bequest amount? _____

Optimal Equity Investing: The Sailboat

1. Fix the mast firmly in place, and set the sails. A broadly diversified, low-cost grouping of funds with overweighting towards the factors that have historically provided higher expected returns (size, value, profitability, dividends, momentum).

2. Keep costs to a minimum (taxes, trading and management).

3. Let the wind do its job.

4. Adjust the sails when needed.

The need to distinguish risk tolerance from risk ability, and to assess each one individually arises from the fact that both can influence outcomes independent of each other. Someone with a high risk tolerance might be psychologically fine with risk, but if they cannot afford to ride out a financial downturn due to income needs or other financial factors, their psychological tolerance to bear risk will be irrelevant—they will nonetheless be forced to sell at the bottom in order to meet their obligations and income needs. Conversely, if someone has a large portfolio and only meager income needs, they may be financially able to ride out a downturn, but if they cannot tolerate the pain psychologically, having the ability to ride out the storm will be irrelevant—they will nonetheless find themselves confronted with an overwhelming desire to sell at the bottom in order to aleviate their inner turmoil.

Invest With (Asset) Class

Studies have shown that more than 90% of investment returns are merely due to asset allocation and not the market-timing or stock-picking approaches most investors are too eager to credit with whatever successes they've had. This means, when we invest, we should really be focusing only on our broader asset allocation decisions (stocks vs bonds, small-cap vs large-cap, etc.). These are the most important decisions.

Once you've settled on your basic allocation between stocks and bonds, it's time to think about your own personal risk-reward preferences* and how they might differ from the average investor considered in the formulas. Once you've decided where you stand, the best place to adjust your portfolio to match your preferences is the stock portion of your portfolio. If you are more risk-averse than the average investor, then you will probably want to keep all of your stock portfolio in broad-based, equal-weighted U.S. index funds. If, on the other hand, you are more willing to take on more risk than the average investor in exchange for greater potential

---

* Here, we are talking about personal risk-reward *preferences* as opposed to the cold hard facts of life circumstances. The latter we use to answer the more basic question of what stock/bond split should we have for our portfolio.

rewards, then you will likely want to take advantage of the research we shared in Chapter 9 and invest in value, small-cap, and international index funds for their tendency to outperform the more popular cap-weighted index funds to an even greater extent than equal-weighted index funds. However, even in this case, it would still be a good idea to hold an equal-weighted, broad-based U.S. stock market index as a core holding or pillar within the stock portion of your portfolio.

Once you've got the right blend of low-cost index funds for your stock portfolio, the next step is to get your bond portfolio in order, if appropriate to your situation. Remember, as we said in Chapter 11, to *make bonds serve you* — and not just your *portfolio plan*, but more importantly, your *life plan*. Your bond portfolio is not going to give you astronomical returns, but it will be there for you if and when you need it. Use either a bond ladder (as discussed in Chapter 11) or some other structure that you have customized to suit the particulars of your life, for example for an anticipated future cash outlay at a known or likely date. Even when bonds are a relatively small part of your portfolio, they still serve an important role as a more immediate and accessible link between your portfolio and the needs of your life. Think of it as though you are painting a portrait where the posing figure is your life. While the bonds are only a small part of the composition, they are a part where it is especially important for you to keep your eyes on the posing figure as you paint the bonds into their proper place.

A *Written* Emergency Plan

While it may sound tedious to take the time to write down an emergency plan, there are at least two very good reasons for doing this. First, by forcing yourself to write out a plan, sentence-by-sentence, you will create a much clearer mental picture of what exactly you should (and will) do in the event of a sudden market downturn or a personal financial emergency. This way, when it happens, it won't feel as though you are going through it for the first time. (For more on the benefits to your mental clarity, read the *"Think!* The Amazon Way" sidebar.) The second reason to write down a plan is so that you can return to it to remind yourself of what you committed yourself to doing in response at a time when you were thinking more clearly.

"Standard economics assumes that we are rational . . . But, as [studies] show, we are far less rational in our decision making . . . Our irrational behaviors are neither random nor senseless—they are systematic and predictable. We all make the same types of mistakes over and over, because of the basic wiring of our brains."

– Dan Ariely, Professor of Psychology and Behavioral Finance
Predictably Irrational

The Fruits of Thinking on Paper

The insights investors have while writing out their emergency plans often include things like remembering an additional source of liquidity ("Oh yeah! I can take out a home equity line of credit if I need a chunk of cash and it's not a good time to sell stocks or bonds."). Or an investor might get a better idea of what, in particular, they find so compelling about the investment strategy they are following. These insights then become a reference list for the tools you have available (that you might otherwise forget) for dealing with personal financial emergencies, and a reference list of the reasons you find most compelling (mental tools) that you can review and revisit during a market downturn to help you weather the storm, instead of panicking and selling at the bottom.

> ## *Think!* the Amazon Way
>
> Amazon founder and CEO, Jeff Bezos, uses writing in his own way to improve the mental clarity of his employees. PowerPoint presentations—where managers can hide behind bullet-point sentence fragments—are banned from meetings, and instead, whoever called the meeting is required to personally write (no assistants allowed) a memorandum explaining why the meeting has been called and what it's purpose is. Before the meeting begins, copies of the memo are handed out to everyone present, and they all take a few silent minutes to read it.
>
> By making Amazon's employees do this (liberal arts majors and engineers alike), they are forced to really think through, sentence-by-sentence, why they are calling the meeting and what they hope to get out of it. As a result, they are much better prepared to lead the meeting and keep it on track.
>
> This is exactly the kind of take-charge, on-track preparedness and mental clarity you will want to have under your belt going into a major market downturn or a personal financial emergency.

A Plan for Sticking to The Plan

One of the best-known stories from *The Odyssey* is the story of Odysseus and the Sirens. The Sirens were dangerous creatures whose beautiful songs and voices would lure sailors to their death on the rocky shores of the island the Sirens inhabited. Odysseus had a plan in place that involved sailing past the Sirens. But he also had a plan for sticking to that plan, so that they would indeed sail past the Sirens and not change course to crash into their shore. He had himself tied to the mast of the boat so that he couldn't move a muscle. And then he told his men to stuff their ears with beeswax and ignore and disobey every one of his orders until they were well beyond the Sirens. It worked! By having a plan for sticking to the plan, he and his sailors were able to avoid disaster.

In a similar way, we must create a plan to bind ourselves (metaphorically speaking) to our overall portfolio plan, including our asset allocation, emergency plan, and the low-cost, long-term, index investing strategies shared in this book. Undoubtedly, the strongest urges to stray off course will come at times when the market Sirens are calling the loudest, i.e. during market downturns. When that happens, we will be tempted to throw our emergency plan out the window, frantically reallocate (or sell out completely), and even forget or discard the very ideas in this book that underpin everything else.

Fortunately, we have already done a great deal of this binding by choosing to follow an investment strategy that has the backing of both common sense and academic rigor. With the support of empirical data, common-sense, and even the reassuring wisdom of Warren Buffett and the like, we can hold fast to our approach as something of a religion. Merriam-Webster defines a religion as "a cause, principle, or system of beliefs held to with ardor." We can hold the system in this book with such ardor by recognizing that it is an empirical and scientific approach to investing, one that has withstood the test of time and the collective wisdom we know as "common sense."

"After spending many years in Wall Street and after making and losing millions of dollars, I want to tell you this: It never was my thinking that made the big money for me. It always was my sitting. Got that? My sitting tight!"

– Jesse Livermore, Stock Trader (1877-1940)
Known as "The Great Bear of Wall Street"

> It's not enough to have a high IQ, to labor long hours, or even get the latest news before everyone else. You must also save yourself from yourself. Like Odysseus and the Sirens, you have to decide first how you're going to tie yourself to the mast of your ship long before the temptations, fears, and anxieties kick in.

You have been armed with the truth about the fees, inefficiencies, and the fallacies that saddle most investors with sub-market returns. And so you are now empowered to free yourself from the tyranny of brokers, compounding costs, and the "great" ideas that will continue to trap unwitting investors for years to come. You now have a strategy and approach that sees the investment world in a clear, organized, and sensible way—one that is backed by research, common-sense, and the wisest investors of our day. And as a result of all this support, it is one that will let you keep your head when all about you are losing theirs. We wish you a secure, empowering, and fulfilling financial future.

The Story of Two Savers

Saver A spends his money partying for 8 years, then opens a tax-deferred account earning 12% at age 26 and invests $150/Month for the next 40 years

Contributions = $72,000

Saver B invests $150/Month for 8 years in a tax-deferred account earning 12% and saves NOTHING for the next 40 years

Contributions = $14,400

Which saver ends up with more money?

Saver A			Saver B		
Age	Annual Amt	Total	Age	Annual Amt	Total
18	$0	$0	18	$1,800	$1,902
19	0	0	19	1,800	4,046
20	0	0	20	1,800	6,462
21	0	0	21	1,800	9,183
22	0	0	22	1,800	12,250
23	0	0	23	1,800	15,706
24	0	0	24	1,800	19,600
25	0	0	25	1,800	23,989
26	1,800	1,902	26	0	26,868
27	1,800	4,046	27	0	30,092
28	1,800	6,462	28	0	33,703
29	1,800	9,183	29	0	37,747
30	1,800	12,250	30	0	42,277
35	1,800	34,506	35	0	74,506
40	1,800	74,937	40	0	131,305
45	1,800	148,388	45	0	231,405
50	1,800	281,827	50	0	407,815
55	1,800	524,245	55	0	718,709
60	1,800	964,644	60	0	1,266,610
65	1,800	1,764,716	65	0	2,232,200

Saver B has outpaced A by over $467,000!!

DON'T PROCRASTINATE

Figure 12-1: Whatever you do, don't wait to get started. A small initial difference of just eight years can make a major difference in the ultimate outcome. Source: RVW Research.

Figure 12-2: This final two-page spread should serve as a summary of the major principles we have covered in this book. Source: Dimensional Fund Advisors.

6 PRACTICE SMART DIVERSIFICATION

Diversification helps reduce risks that have no expected return, but diversifying within your home market is not enough. Global diversification can broaden your investment universe.

Home Market Index Portfolio

S&P 500 Index
1 COUNTRY,
500 STOCKS

Global Market Index Portfolio

MSCI ACWI
Investable Market
Index (IMI)
46 COUNTRIES,
8,628 STOCKS

7 AVOID MARKET TIMING

You never know which market segments will outperform from year to year. By holding a globally diversified portfolio, investors are well positioned to seek returns wherever they occur.

Annual Returns by Market Index

US Large Cap
US Large Cap Value
US Small Cap
US Small Cap Value
US Real Estate
Intl. Large Cap Value
Intl. Small Cap Value
Emerging Markets
Five-Year US Govt. Fixed

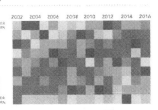

8 MANAGE YOUR EMOTIONS

Many people struggle to separate their emotions from investing. Markets go up and down. Reacting to current market conditions may lead to making poor investment decisions.

Avoid Reactive Investing

ELATION

NERVOUSNESS   OPTIMISM

OPTIMISM

FEAR

9 LOOK BEYOND THE HEADLINES

Daily market news and commentary can challenge your investment discipline. Some messages stir anxiety about the future, while others tempt you to chase the latest investment fad. When headlines unsettle you, consider the source and maintain a long-term perspective.

RETIRE RICH

SELL STOCKS NOW!

THE LOOMING RECESSION

THE TOP 10 FUNDS TO OWN

MARKET HITS RECORD HIGH!

HOUSING MARKET BOOM!

10 FOCUS ON WHAT YOU CAN CONTROL

A financial advisor can offer expertise and guidance to help you focus on actions that add value. This can lead to a better investment experience.

- Create an investment plan to fit your needs and risk tolerance
- Structure a portfolio along the dimensions of expected returns
- Diversify globally
- Manage expenses, turnover, and taxes
- Stay disciplined through market dips and swings

A Word on Inflation

Many investors find themselves worrying about inflation. With the currently large U.S. budget deficits and the Federal Reserve's easy monetary policy, there is in fact a real chance we could see some significant inflation in the near future. As Professor Jeremy J. Siegel points out:

> "Inflation is the insidious, though technically legal, way in which the government defaults on its obligations."

And so, the government itself may actually *want* inflation in order to lower its obligations in this kind of "technical default."

Nonetheless, investors following the approach outlined in this book have little cause for concern. When we take a 30-year time horizon and look at the returns on stocks after taking into account the effects of inflation, we find that stock returns have been virtually unaffected by periods of inflation. The prices of goods and services, as measured by the Consumer Price Index, has risen elevenfold since January 1947. Meanwhile, the S&P 500® Index, valued at 15.66 in January 1947, reached 2272 in December 2016—*140 times higher!*

During the inflationary postwar period the real return on stocks was almost exactly the same as it had been in the nineteenth and early-twentieth centuries—a time when inflation was virtually nonexistent. And for those relying on the income from their investments, consider the following: stock dividends have risen faster than inflation both in periods of slowly rising prices *and* in periods of rapidly rising prices.

Acknowledgments

First and foremost, we would like to thank our clients at RVW Wealth for placing their trust in us through the years. Knowing that your financial health and well-being depends largely on each decision we make gives our decisions a sense of gravity and seriousness that has helped make us that much better. We are grateful for the opportunity to serve you.

We would also like to thank our team at RVW Wealth for your hard, dedicated work and for the incredible sense of character each one of you brings to work each day. You truly make our work into one of the great joys in our lives. Special thanks to our esteemed colleague, Stephen Seo, CPA, CFA, who helps guide the RVW ship as one of our key team members.

Though a bit premature, we would also like to thank anyone who has taken the time to read this book. After all, it is because of you that this book was written. We cannot possibly serve every investor on the planet, and it was with you in mind that this book found its purpose.

We should also thank our editor, Donovan Schafer, for his careful edits and thoughtful additions. It has truly been a pleasure to work with him. We would also like to extend our sincere thanks to Cheston Mizel and Larry Weinman for their invaluable contribution.

And last but not least, we would like to thank our families. In the end, you are what makes all this possible. You are why we get up in the morning and why we want to make the world a better place. We don't want you living in a world filled with villains who want to stand in the way of your financial well-being. We want you to live and love without these burdens and distractions. It has been said that "Those who fight for the future live in it today." Fighting for that future, for you, in writing this book, has allowed us to glimpse that future, and makes us feel excitement, joy, and gratitude for the future we hope you will enjoy.

Appendix

Bond Trading Transaction Costs

No matter where you decide to buy or sell your bonds, you should be prepared to pay a transaction cost. The costs you will pay depend on the market on which you buy your bonds.

The difference between the price a broker-dealer pays for a bond and the price at which it is sold to you is known as the bond's markup. The markup is a transaction cost. With new issues, the broker-dealer's markup is included in the par value, so you do not pay separate transaction costs.

Everyone who buys a new issue pays the same price, known as the offering price. If you are interested in a new issue, you can get an offering statement describing the bond's features and risks.

Instead of charging you a commission to perform the transaction for you, the broker-dealer marks up the price of the bond to above its face value. When you buy or sell bonds through a broker-dealer on the secondary market, the bonds will have price markups. Instead of charging you a commission to perform the transaction for you, the broker-dealer marks up the price of the bond to above its face value. Markups are usually from about 1% - 5% of the bond's original value. Bond dealers generally charge higher markups on smaller bond sales than larger ones. If you are buying a Treasury bond over the counter, you may have to pay a small, additional flat fee.

If you sell a bond before it matures, you may receive more or less than the par value of the bond. Either way, your broker-dealer will mark down the price of your bond, paying you slightly less than its current value. He or she will then mark up the price slightly upon resale to another investor. This is how broker-dealers are compensated for maintaining this active secondary market.

Bonds bought on the exchanges generally have much higher markups than bonds bought over the counter. It is difficult to know how much of a markup you are paying, because the markup is built into the price of the bond.

Weather vs. Climate

Have you noticed how TV news bulletins place finance next to the weather report? In each, talking heads point at charts and intone about intra-day events that are quickly forgotten. Meanwhile, the long-term wealth-building story gets overlooked. Human beings love stories. But this innate tendency can lead us to imagine connections between events where none really exist and derive universal patterns from what are really just random events. Sadly, this linking of news events to short-term stock price movements can lead us to think that if we study the news closely enough, we can work out which way the market will move.

> *Human beings are meaning-making machines, seeking to find patterns where there are none. Randomness is simply too complex for most to internalize.*

Building neat and tidy stories out of short-term price changes might be a good way to win ratings and readership, but it is not a good way to approach investing, and it causes many investors to feel that they are not properly informed about the financial world unless they have checked daily, or even hourly, on how the Dow, FTSE or Nikkei have moved in the intervening period. Our very human focus on the day-to-day encourages us to make bad decisions that affect our long-term interests. That's because while we live moment to moment, what often affects us most are imperceptible, gradual changes that occur over many years.

Watching animals in the wild shows us what our instincts are —to "herd" when we feel safe and to "flee" when we sense danger. That will cause us to want to sell when everyone is panicking and the market is in free-fall, and to want to buy when everyone else is buying. Our impulse is therefore to sell at or near the bottom and to buy when the market is most frothy. The greatest challenge, therefore, is to suppress natural impulses and to view market movements with equanimity. *Look at the following five famous predictions of pundits and investors that went badly awry:*

- In the 1920s, Yale University's Irving Fisher was a household name in America and by far its best-known economist; his pronouncements regularly made front-page headlines. **Three days before the crash of 1929**, he famously announced that "stock prices have reached what appears to be a permanently high plateau"—and for months after the crash, he maintained that a recovery in stock prices was imminent.

- In 1980 and 1981, Joe Granville's investment seminars drew packed audiences, and his predictions caused major one-day moves in the market. Granville even predicted that he would win the Nobel Prize in economics; and on one occasion he literally walked on water, as he made his entrance strolling across a swimming pool that he'd filled with concrete. But according to the Hulbert Report, which tracks the performance of investment newsletters, from 1980 to 2005 The Granville Letter was dead last among American newsletters, with **investors who followed its advice losing 95% of their capital**.

- In 1987, Elliott Wave proponent Robert Prechter told clients to sell in advance of Black Monday: He's been cashing in on that call ever since and, in the process, **told his readers to stay on the sidelines throughout the record bull market of the 1990s.**

- In 2000, Merrill Lynch tech guru Henry Blodget **predicted that tech valuations would continue to climb**—and backed up his words by putting his personal net worth on the line, most of which was lost.

- John A. Paulson made more than $15 billion for his hedge funds by betting on the collapse of the mortgage-backed securities market in 2007 and 2008. In 2011, Paulson's ironically named Advantage Plus fund **suffered a 52 percent decline**, its worst in the firm's 17-year history. In January 2016, Paulson was forced to put up his own investments as additional collateral for a credit line with HSBC and his love of the health-care sector, particularly a little company called Valeant Pharmaceuticals, was reason alone to close his office door, draw the blinds, and weep.

Long-term equity investors should not be in the business of making predictions or taking big bets in one direction or another. They seek to be fractional owners of a diverse group of quality businesses and are constantly sifting the noise from the news. To use an analogy, the market news is like the weather. One day it's sunny, the next day it rains. It's unseasonably warm one day but cool the next. The narrower your frame of reference is, the greater the apparent variability.

"Investing is not a 110-meter race. It is a marathon. If you want to finish the race, you shouldn't try to go faster; you should slow down. And you need to learn how to resist investing in any asset or strategy you don't understand."

– Jason Zweig, Columnist, *Wall Street Journal*
"The Intelligent Investor"

Focusing on the long term, be less concerned with the day-to-day movements and more on how wealth accumulates through time. For the serious investor, this is the more important measure because it considers cumulative gains—and the power of compounding growth (especially in a tax-deferred manner). The media, by virtue of their publication schedule, must focus on the short-term. They need a different story every day.

These two ways of looking at the market are like the difference between the weather and the climate. The former changes constantly, the latter more gradually. With long-term investment, it's the climate you need to think about.

The Evolution of a New Kind of Financial Advisor: Beyond Economic Predictions and Market Forecasts

Here are the six hats your advisor should wear to help you, without ever having to look into a crystal ball:

1. **The Fiduciary:** Many wealth managers observe a "suitability" duty of care rather than the role of a true fiduciary. Your advisor should place your interests ahead of their own and have interests that are fully aligned with yours. They take no undisclosed commissions or incentives and keep fees ultra-low. The global financial turmoil of recent years demonstrated the value of an independent and objective voice in a world full of product pushers and salespeople whose interests are frequently in direct conflict with yours.

2. **The Expert:** Now, more than ever, investors need advisors who can provide client-centered expertise in assessing the state of their finances and developing risk-aware strategies to help them meet their goals — and who have the training and experience in the affiliated areas of economics, finance and taxes which are needed in today's complex environment to provide holistic financial advice. It's about process not product.

3. **The Architect:** A good advisor will listen to the clients' fears, tease out the issues driving those feelings, and provide practical, long-term answers that respond to each client's needs for income, growth and safety respectively. A long-term wealth management strategy will match each client's risk tolerance and lifetime goals.

4. **The Teacher:** Getting beyond the fear-and-flight phase often is just a matter of teaching investors about risk and

return, volatility, diversification, the role of asset allocation, and the virtue of discipline.

5. **The Coach**: Even when the strategy is in place, doubts and fears inevitably arise. At this point, the advisor becomes a coach, reinforcing first principles and keeping the client on track especially during down markets when many tend to question the wisdom of their chosen strategy.

6. **The Guardian**: Beyond these experiences is a long-term role for the advisor as a kind of lighthouse keeper, scanning the horizon for issues that may affect the client and keeping them informed.

IT'S ALL ABOUT TRUST AND EXPERTISE: Knowing that your advisor is independent—and not plugging product—leads to trust. However you characterize these various roles, good financial advice ultimately is defined by the patient building of a long-term relationship founded on the values of trust and integrity. **Now, how can you put a price on that? Remember: Good advice doesn't cost. It pays.**

I, Pencil

My Family Tree as told to Leonard E. Read

I am a lead pencil—the ordinary wooden pencil familiar to all boys and girls and adults who can read and write.

Writing is both my vocation and my avocation; that's all I do.

You may wonder why I should write a genealogy. Well, to begin with, my story is interesting. And, next, I am a mystery—more so than a tree or a sunset or even a flash of lightning. But, sadly, I am taken for granted by those who use me, as if I were a mere incident and without background. This supercilious attitude relegates me to the level of the commonplace. This is a species of the grievous error in which mankind cannot too long persist without peril. For, the wise G. K. Chesterton observed, "We are perishing for want of wonder, not for want of wonders."

I, Pencil, simple though I appear to be, merit your wonder and awe, a claim I shall attempt to prove. In fact, if you can understand me—no, that's too much to ask of anyone—if you can become aware of the miraculousness which I symbolize, you can help save the freedom mankind is so unhappily losing. I have a profound lesson to teach. And I can teach this lesson better than can an automobile or an airplane or a mechanical dishwasher because—well, because I am seemingly so simple.

Simple? Yet, *not a single person on the face of this earth knows how to make me.* This sounds fantastic, doesn't it? Especially when it is realized that there are about one and one-half billion of my kind produced in the U.S.A. each year.

Pick me up and look me over. What do you see? Not much meets the eye—there's some wood, lacquer, the printed labeling, graphite lead, a bit of metal, and an eraser.

Innumerable Antecedents

Just as you cannot trace your family tree back very far, so is it impossible for me to name and explain all my antecedents. But I would like to suggest enough of them to impress upon you the richness and complexity of my background.

My family tree begins with what in fact is a tree, a cedar of straight grain that grows in Northern California and Oregon. Now contemplate all the saws and trucks and rope and the countless other gear used in harvesting and carting the cedar logs to the railroad siding. Think of all the persons and the numberless skills that went into their fabrication: the mining of ore, the making of steel and its refinement into saws, axes, motors; the growing of hemp and bringing it through all the stages to heavy and strong rope; the logging camps with their beds and mess halls, the cookery and the raising of all the foods. Why, untold thousands of persons had a hand in every cup of coffee the loggers drink!

The logs are shipped to a mill in San Leandro, California. Can you imagine the individuals who make flat cars and rails and railroad engines and who construct and install the communication systems incidental thereto? These legions are among my antecedents.

Consider the millwork in San Leandro. The cedar logs are cut into small, pencil-length slats less than one-fourth of an inch in thickness. These are kiln dried and then tinted for the same reason women put rouge on their faces. People prefer that I look pretty, not a pallid white. The slats are waxed and kiln dried again. How many skills went into the making of the tint and the kilns, into supplying the heat, the light and power, the belts, motors, and all the other things a mill requires? Sweepers in the mill among my ancestors? Yes, and included are the men who poured the concrete for the dam of a Pacific Gas & Electric Company hydroplant which supplies the mill's power!

Don't overlook the ancestors present and distant who have a hand in transporting sixty carloads of slats across the nation.

Once in the pencil factory—$4,000,000 in machinery and building, all capital accumulated by thrifty and saving parents of mine—each slat is given eight grooves by a complex machine, after which another machine lays leads in every other slat, applies glue, and places another slat atop—a lead sandwich, so to speak. Seven brothers and I are mechanically carved from this "wood-clinched" sandwich.

My "lead" itself—it contains no lead at all—is complex. The graphite is mined in Ceylon. Consider these miners and those who make their many tools and the makers of the paper sacks in which the graphite is shipped and those who make the string that ties the sacks and those who put them aboard ships and those who make the ships. Even the lighthouse keepers along the way assisted in my birth—and the harbor pilots.

The graphite is mixed with clay from Mississippi in which ammonium hydroxide is used in the refining process. Then wetting agents are added such as sulfonated tallow—animal fats chemically reacted with sulfuric acid. After passing through numerous machines, the mixture finally appears as endless extrusions—as from a sausage grinder-cut to size, dried, and baked for several hours at 1,850 degrees Fahrenheit. To increase their strength and smoothness the leads are then treated with a hot mixture which includes candelilla wax from Mexico, paraffin wax, and hydrogenated natural fats.

My cedar receives six coats of lacquer. Do you know all the ingredients of lacquer? Who would think that the growers of castor beans and the refiners of castor oil are a part of it? They are. Why, even the processes by which the lacquer is made a beautiful yellow involve the skills of more persons than one can enumerate!

Observe the labeling. That's a film formed by applying heat to carbon black mixed with resins. How do you make resins and what, pray, is carbon black?

My bit of metal—the ferrule—is brass. Think of all the persons who mine zinc and copper and those who have the skills to make shiny sheet brass from these products of nature. Those black rings on my ferrule are black nickel. What is black nickel and how is it applied? The complete story of why the center of my ferrule has no black nickel on it would take pages to explain.

Then there's my crowning glory, inelegantly referred to in the trade as "the plug," the part man uses to erase the errors he makes with me. An ingredient called "factice" is what does the erasing. It is a rubber-like product made by reacting rape-seed oil from the Dutch East Indies with sulfur chloride. Rubber, contrary to the common notion, is only for binding purposes. Then, too, there are numerous vulcanizing and accelerating agents. The pumice comes from Italy; and the pigment which gives "the plug" its color is cadmium sulfide.

No One Knows

Does anyone wish to challenge my earlier assertion that no single person on the face of this earth knows how to make me?

Actually, millions of human beings have had a hand in my creation, no one of whom even knows more than a very few of the others. Now, you may say that I go too far in relating the picker of a coffee berry in far off Brazil and food growers elsewhere to my creation; that this is an extreme position. I shall stand by my claim. There isn't a single person in all these millions, including the president of the pencil company, who contributes more than a tiny, infinitesimal bit of know-how. From the standpoint of know-how the only difference between the miner of graphite in Ceylon and the logger in Oregon is in the *type* of know-how. Neither the miner nor the logger can be dispensed with, any more than can the chemist at the factory or the worker in the oil field—paraffin being a by-product of petroleum.

Here is an astounding fact: Neither the worker in the oil field nor the chemist nor the digger of graphite or clay nor any who mans or makes the ships or trains or trucks nor the one who runs the machine that does the knurling on my bit of metal nor the president of the company performs his singular task because he wants me. Each one wants me less, perhaps, than does a child in the first grade. Indeed, there are some among this vast multitude who never saw a pencil nor would they know how to use one. Their motivation is other than me. Perhaps it is something like this: Each of these millions sees that he can thus exchange his tiny know-how for the goods and services he needs or wants. I may or may not be among these items.

No Master Mind

There is a fact still more astounding: the absence of a master mind, of anyone dictating or forcibly directing these countless actions which bring me into being. No trace of such a person can be found. Instead, we find the Invisible Hand at work. This is the mystery to which I earlier referred.

It has been said that "only God can make a tree." Why do we agree with this? Isn't it because we realize that we ourselves could not make one? Indeed, can we even describe a tree? We cannot, except in superficial terms. We can say, for instance, that a certain molecular configuration manifests itself as a tree. But what mind is there among men that could even record, let alone direct, the constant changes in molecules that transpire in the life span of a tree? Such a feat is utterly unthinkable!

I, Pencil, am a complex combination of miracles: a tree, zinc, copper, graphite, and so on. But to these miracles which manifest themselves in Nature an even more extraordinary miracle has been added: the configuration of creative human energies—millions of tiny know-hows configurating naturally and spontaneously in response to human necessity and desire and *in the absence of any human master-minding!* Since only God can make a tree, I insist that only God could make me. Man can no more direct these millions of know-hows to bring me into being than he can put molecules together to create a tree.

The above is what I meant when writing, "If you can become aware of the miraculousness which I symbolize, you can help save the freedom mankind is so unhappily losing." For, if one is aware that these know-hows will naturally, yes, automatically, arrange themselves into creative and productive patterns in response to human necessity and demand—that is, in the absence of governmental or any other coercive masterminding—then one will possess an absolutely essential ingredient for freedom: *a faith in free people.* Freedom is impossible without this faith.

Once government has had a monopoly of a creative activity such, for instance, as the delivery of the mails, most individuals will believe that the mails could not be efficiently delivered by men acting freely. And here is the reason: Each one acknowledges that he himself doesn't know how to do all the things incident to mail delivery. He also recognizes that no other individual could do it. These assumptions are correct. No individual possesses enough know-how to perform a nation's mail delivery any more than any individual possesses enough know-how to make a pencil. Now, in the absence of faith in free people—in the unawareness that millions of tiny know-hows would naturally and miraculously form and cooperate to satisfy this necessity — the individual cannot help but reach the erroneous conclusion that mail can be delivered only by governmental "master-minding."

Testimony Galore

If I, Pencil, were the only item that could offer testimony on what men and women can accomplish when free to try, then those with little faith would have a fair case. However, there is testimony galore; it's all about us and on every hand. Mail delivery is exceedingly simple when compared, for instance, to the making of an automobile or a calculating machine or a grain combine or a milling machine or to tens of thousands of other things. Delivery? Why, in this area where men have been left free to try, they deliver the human voice around the world in less than one second; they deliver an event visually and in motion to any person's home when it is happening; they deliver 150 passengers from Seattle to Baltimore in less than four hours; they deliver gas from Texas to one's range or furnace in New York at unbelievably low rates and without subsidy; they deliver each four pounds of oil from the Persian Gulf to our Eastern Seaboard — halfway around the world — for less money than the government charges for delivering a one-ounce letter across the street!

The lesson I have to teach is this: *Leave all creative energies uninhibited.* Merely organize society to act in harmony with this lesson. Let society's legal apparatus remove all obstacles the best it can. Permit these creative know-hows freely to flow. Have faith that free men and women will respond to the Invisible Hand. This faith will be confirmed. I, Pencil, seemingly simple though I am, offer the miracle of my creation as testimony that this is a practical faith, as practical as the sun, the rain, a cedar tree, the good earth.

Leonard E. Read (1898-1983) founded FEE in 1946 and served as its president until his death.

"I, Pencil," his most famous essay, was first published in the December 1958 issue of **The Freeman.** *Although a few of the manufacturing details and place names have changed over the past forty years, the principles are unchanged.*

The 'CAPE' Mistake

[Why the most popular stock market valuation measure is flawed]

While it's popular today to point to the CAPE ratio (also known as the "Shiller PE ratio") as proof that the market is overvalued, those who do rarely understand the ratio, its origins, and its limitations. Other metrics arrive at the same conclusion—as screaming headlines point out almost daily in the media and blogosphere—based on equally irrelevant information.

Despite being popularized by a Nobel Prize-winning economist (Robert Shiller) the CAPE ratio itself involves no complex calculations, advanced economic theories, or adjustments for current economic conditions. It is a simple and crude measure that even a first-grader could calculate: current stock price for the S&P 500 companies divided by the 10-year average of their historical earnings-per-share (adjusted for inflation). That's it. Nothing more.

Figure 1: The CAPE Ratio

This graph shows the CAPE (Cyclically Adjusted Price to Earnings) ratio from 1881 to the present. Source: http://www.multpl.com/shiller-pe/

Understanding 'CAPE'

Shiller got the idea of using a 10-year average for earnings from Benjamin Graham (Warren Buffett's mentor) who used such an average to capture what he referred to as "earnings power" in his 1934 book *Security Analysis*. Graham knew that reported earnings could go up and down; but, he felt that the underlying business possessed a more fundamental characteristic that he called its "earnings power." This was essentially the business's inherent *capacity* to generate earnings, notwithstanding the vagaries of quarterly and annual reporting. He used the trailing average earnings as a way to approximate this "earnings power." However, Graham himself warned against using this measure as a "mere arithmetical" calculation and emphasized the need to consider the broader context to determine whether using an average was really appropriate given the circumstances. And, in today's market, context is everything.

For starters, using a 10-year trailing average made sense in Graham's day, when American business was dominated by slowing-growing manufacturers, but it makes far less sense in the faster-moving world of today, where companies can make more meaningful changes in a span of less than ten years. Can Google's earnings from ten years ago really tell us anything meaningful about its true "earnings power" today? What's more, stretching the average out across 10 years forces us to include the worst recession since The Great Depression. Unless you think this once-in-a-century event actually says something meaningful about the true "earnings power" (the capacity) of American businesses, it doesn't make sense to include this in the calculation. These effects artificially drag down earnings, distorting them and inflating the CAPE ratio.

Graham, an astute observer of accounting practices, no doubt would have noticed another factor that would need to be considered before blindly applying the CAPE ratio as a "mere arithmetical" calculation. In 1990, there was a change in standard accounting practices that required companies to markdown their assets and record losses (lowering earnings) whenever those assets lost value, yet when these same assets increased in value the companies were only allowed to record gains (increasing earnings) when, if ever, they sold these assets. The net effect was to create an overall downward pressure on reported earnings, and therefore an upward pressure on the computed CAPE ratio. It should come as no surprise, therefore, that the CAPE ratio shows a persistently overvalued market after 1990.

The Historical Test

To see the effects of these distortions, let's consider what would have happened if someone had actually adhered to the CAPE ratio, warts and all, during the past three decades? The long-term average for the CAPE ratio, going back 134 years, is roughly 16. If you had waited for the CAPE ratio to tell you the market was "undervalued" by falling below 16, you would have jumped into the market only twice (1987 and 2009), each time jumping back out only a year or two later when the market would be "overvalued" again. You would have missed most of the 1990s bull market, the 2002-2007 bull market, and the incredible gains of the past five years. Conversely, a simple buy-and-hold strategy of a typical broad market index fund during this period would have yielded well over 800%.

Perhaps the greatest weakness of the CAPE ratio is that it does not take into account today's ultra-low interest rates. But that brings us to the CAPE ratio's alternatives—those based on the theories of modern finance and not resurrected ideas from the

1930s. The key distinction of modern finance is that it appreciates the importance of *relative* pricing across asset classes. While Graham focused on relating each stock to its "earnings power" in isolation, modern finance seeks to integrate all asset classes (stocks, corporate bonds, government securities, mortgages, etc.) through the unifying lens of interest rates and earnings yields (the stock equivalent of an interest rate).

Rather than looking at stock prices in isolation, another theory known as the Fed Theory recognizes that investors have a choice between stocks and bonds. And not surprisingly, since they can alternate back and forth between these two options, the two types of investments tend to have very similar yields (i.e. interest rates for bonds and earnings yields for stocks). Figure 2 shows the 10-year treasury yield and the earnings yield for the S&P 500. One can see easily, just from looking at the chart, how closely the two yields follow each other.

Figure 2: S&P 500 Earnings Yield vs 10-Year Treasury Yield

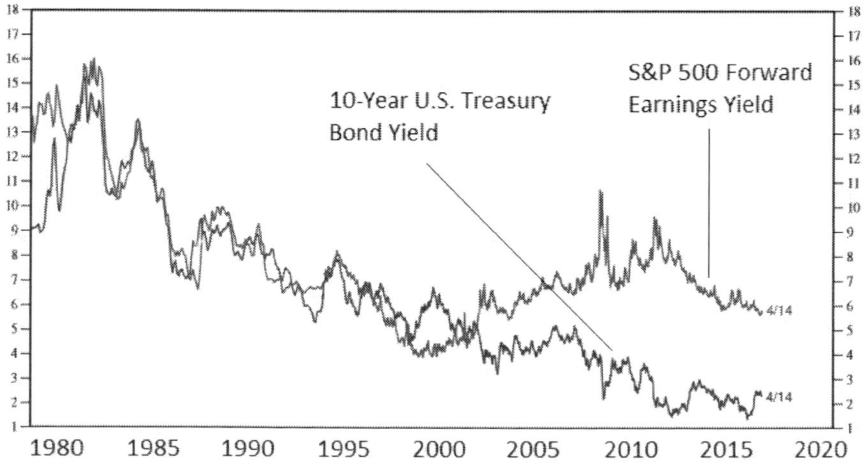

This graph shows the forward earnings yield for the S&P 500 and the yield for the 10-year U.S. Treasury Note from 1979 to April 14, 2017.

'Stacked In Favor Of The Bulls'

But there's another important feature to notice in the figure. Since 2010, the S&P 500 earnings yield has been significantly higher than the 10-year treasury yield. There is a lingering gap that has yet to be closed. In order to close this gap, we need lower earnings, higher stock prices, or both (since the earnings yield is earnings divided by the stock price). We believe it unlikely that corporate earnings will decline or interest rates will climb significantly, *making the bullish case* for equity prices as the equilibrating factor in this relationship and restoring their historic relative ratios.

If stock prices go higher, it's a clear win for investors. But if earnings go lower, it is neither a clear win nor a clear loss for investors. Sure, lower earnings could lead to lower stock prices, but because stock prices are in the denominator they cannot fall faster than the earnings — otherwise the fall in stock prices would offset the effect of the fall in earnings and the gap in Figure 2 wouldn't close at all. This effectively puts a limit on how far and how fast stock prices can actually fall. From this perspective, the deck is really stacked in favor of those who expect to see a rise in stock prices and limits the downside.

Not only is the deck stacked in favor of the bulls, but the payout could be quite substantial. Looking again at Figure 2, the last time there was this much of a pricing discrepancy between stocks and bonds (represented by the gap) was in the late 1970s. Many investors, including Warren Buffett, look back on this period fondly, remembering it as the "good old days" when they were able to scoop up the stocks that gave them handsome returns through the 1980s and 1990s.

Conclusion

It would be a grave mistake—*a CAPE mistake*—to miss this kind of opportunity simply because we were too dazzled by the popularity of the stock metric *du jur*. History is solidly on the side of the bulls, and it is likely that—for those who can tolerate severe turbulence—the rewards will be abundant.

Guide your investment ship by the stars and not by the prevailing winds.

The Five Investment Perennials

(They happen every year...)

1. Investors will buy high and sell low. Most will follow the herds—in and out of the market.

As always, most investors will do the wrong thing at the wrong time. If stocks go up, they will buy. If stocks decline, they will sell. In short, investors will be predictably irrational, as opposed to sticking to an investment allocation they can live with and which is responsive to their needs for income, safety and growth. The problem is that we are genetically programmed to be bad investors—we flee when we sense danger, and crowd when we feel comfortable. Being a savvy investor means being willing to stand apart from the crowd and from group-think. Warren Buffett cautions: "Be greedy when others are fearful—and fearful when others are greedy".

2. The hottest investment will gather the most money.

Something will be hot, and investors will pour their money into it. Whether digital currency, gold, hedge funds, a new flavor of fund, master limited partnerships or stocks of a certain industry, billions of dollars will be flowing into that hot investment after the price has skyrocketed, after which the price will keep soaring—for a while. The hot performance will then cool, and those who poured their hard-earned money into this sure bet will be disappointed. Flavor-of-the-month is good for ice creams—not for investing. Beware the new fund flavor being marketed.

3. Financial gurus will brag about their winners and not mention their losers.

The investing public will be inundated by videos, web stories and other media in which financial gurus will tout their winners and look brilliant doing so. You will wish you had followed their advice, but be careful what you wish for. They are almost certainly not mentioning their losers. Any fund family with 50 or more funds will be able to point to a couple that did very well.

4. A new paradigm will be born.

Since the year 2000, we've had a few particularly dangerous and costly new paradigms:

- A company's cash flow no longer matters. (The internet stock bubble.)
- Real estate can never decline. (The real estate bubble.)
- Capitalism is dead. (The real estate and financial crisis of 2008-09.)
- Stocks only move up. (The bull market following 20009.)

Nature abhors a vacuum, and the nature of investing is no different. It won't be long before another patently ridiculous paradigm rushes in to fill the void. That new paradigm will ultimately prove to be false, of course. And with the benefit of hindsight and investing amnesia, we'll marvel at everyone else's silliness.

5. You will be pitched something with high returns and low risk.

Special opportunities will be available to only a select few, and you may even need to decide that day. The pitch will be irresistible. However, if you first ask yourself why they need to pay someone to pitch it to you as a small investor, rather than being snapped up by large investors or institutions, then you will save yourself a lot of buyer's remorse and heartburn from the likely financial loss. Ask anyone who invested in the Madoff fund.

Seven Ways to Fool Yourself

We delude ourselves for a number of reasons, but one of the principal causes is a need to protect our own egos. So we look for external evidence that supports the myths we hold about ourselves, and we dismiss those facts that are incompatible.

Psychologists call this "confirmation bias"—a tendency to select facts that suit our own internal beliefs. A related ingrained tendency, known as "hindsight bias," involves seeing everything as obvious and predictable after the fact.

These biases, or ways of protecting our egos from reality, are evident among many investors every day and are often encouraged by the media.

Here are seven common manifestations of how investors fool themselves:

1. "Everyone could see that market crash coming." Have you noticed how people become experts after the fact? But if "everyone" could see a correction coming, why wasn't "everyone" profiting from it? You don't need forecasts.

2. "I only invest in 'blue-chip' companies." People often gravitate to the familiar and to shares they see as solid. But a company's profile and whether or not it is a good investment are not necessarily correlated. Better to diversify.

3. "I'm waiting for more certainty." The emotions triggered by volatility are understandable, but acting on those emotions can be counterproductive. Uncertainty goes with investing. Historically, long-term discipline has been rewarded.

4. "I know about this industry, so I'm going to buy the stock." People often assume that success in investment requires a specialist's knowledge of a sector. But that information is usually already in the price. Trust the market instead. The philosopher Ludwig Wittgenstein once said that nothing is as difficult for people as not deceiving themselves. But while most self-delusions are relatively costless, those relating to investment can come with a hefty price tag.

5. "It was still a good call, but no one saw this coming." Isn't that the point? You can rationalize a stock-specific bet as much as you like, but events or external influences can conspire against you. Spread your risk instead.

6. "I'm going to restrict my portfolio to the strongest economies." If an economy performs strongly, that will no doubt be reflected in stock prices. What moves prices is news. And news relates to the unexpected. So work with the market.

7. "OK, it was a bad idea, but I don't want to sell at a loss." We can put too much faith in individual stocks, and holding onto a losing bet can mean missing opportunities elsewhere. Portfolio structure affects performance.

This is by no means an exhaustive list. In fact, the capacity for human beings to delude themselves in the world of investment is never-ending.

But overcoming self-deception is not impossible. It just starts with recognizing that, as humans, we are not wired for disciplined investing. We will always find one way or another of rationalizing an emotional reaction to market events.

But that's why even experienced investors engage advisors who know them, and who understand their circumstances, risk appetites, and long-term goals. The role of that advisor is to listen to and acknowledge our very human fears, while keeping us in the plans we committed to at our most lucid and logical.

We will always try to fool ourselves. But to quote a piece of folk wisdom, the essence of self-discipline is to do the important thing rather than the urgent thing.

The Mindset Needed to be a Successful Long-Term Equity Investor

"We position the sails optimally and let the wind do its job."

A market without volatility would be unnatural, like an ocean without waves. The free market, like the open ocean, is constantly churning. For some investors, market-moving waves can be exciting, providing a buying opportunity for mispriced securities. For other investors, the waves might feel violent; but truthfully, for long-term investors, market volatility should be irrelevant.

> A smooth sea never made a skilled sailor.

The degree of market volatility varies from small ripples, to rolling waves, to a financial crisis-sized tsunami. While all volatility feels uncomfortable in the near term, the important question for long-term investors is how to respond to it. In this bulletin, we outline four principles that will help investors navigate a choppy market.

Expect bigger waves

We are entering the later stages of a long economic expansion. While we expect a healthy, growing economy in the coming year, it is important to acknowledge that volatility tends to be elevated in the second half of the business cycle. To expand upon our nautical metaphor, we liken the cyclical nature of volatility to the ocean tide. Volatility ebbs with the positive and steadfast economic news that characterizes the beginning of the business cycle, and it flows when the market is mired by slowing economic momentum and fears of recession. Exhibit 1 illustrates this concept over the previous three business cycles.

Skittish investors who are skeptical of the prospects of future economic growth are the main cause of the bigger waves at the end of the cycle. When there are fears of a recession, investors' "edge of seat" mentality causes quick and sometimes irrational decision making, and the subsequent herd behavior can amplify the market drawdown and ultimately cause tsunami-magnitude volatility.

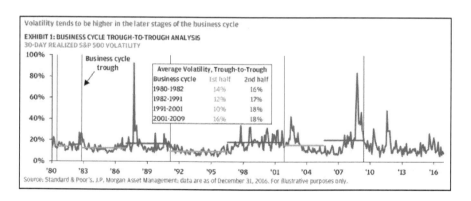

Grab an oar! Here is what you will need to do...

Actually, as a long-term investor you'll need to do less than you think. Your diversified portfolio was built to feel steady in rough seas.

1. Remember that volatility is normal.

Volatility in the market is normal, and feeling uneasy about a lower portfolio value is normal too. Illustrating how often investors experience moderate pullbacks is simple enough. Exhibit 2 depicts the number of 5% pullbacks experienced each year. The chart reminds us that even in years with outstanding equity returns, there are rolling waves of volatility in the market. What we cannot show in a chart is the seasickness an investor feels while riding these waves to a lower portfolio value.

Historical analysis shows that pullbacks of 5% have occurred about once a quarter, and pullbacks of 10% are likely to occur once per year. Large pullbacks greater than 20% tend to occur just once per market cycle. A savvy investor will recognize the high frequency of equity market volatility, and will determine the source of the volatility before reacting to it.

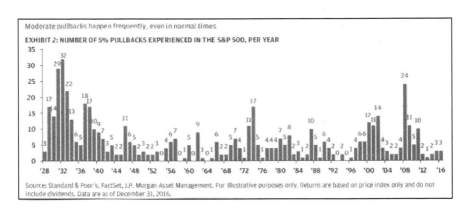

Moderate pullbacks happen frequently, even in normal times

EXHIBIT 2: NUMBER OF 5% PULLBACKS EXPERIENCED IN THE S&P 500, PER YEAR

Source: Standard & Poor's, FactSet, J.P. Morgan Asset Management. For illustrative purposes only. Returns are based on price index only and do not include dividends. Data are as of December 31, 2016.

2. Do not jump ship at the bottom: Markets tend to rebound after bouts of volatility.

Focusing on the long-term trends of the market rather than the short-term gyrations should give investors the confidence to ride the waves of volatility. When examining historic equity market data, we see a trend of rebounds following equity market pullbacks. That means that investors who jump ship after a big wave may have broken the cardinal rule of investing by "selling low."

Exhibit 3 shows the largest intra-year decline and the calendar year return every year since 1980. Despite an average intra-year drop of 14.2%, the market ended the year higher than it began it 76% of the time. That is why it is important for investors to ride the wave of volatility through its full cycle.

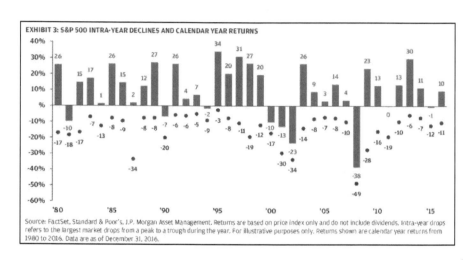

EXHIBIT 3: S&P 500 INTRA-YEAR DECLINES AND CALENDAR YEAR RETURNS

Source: FactSet, Standard & Poor's, J.P. Morgan Asset Management. Returns are based on price index only and do not include dividends. Intra-year drops refers to the largest market drops from a peak to a trough during the year. For illustrative purposes only. Returns shown are calendar year returns from 1980 to 2016. Data are as of December 31, 2016.

We recognize some of the deep market pullbacks in Exhibit 3. The pullback of nearly 50% in 2008, for example, occurred in the wake of the global financial crisis. And the three consecutive years of negative returns in the early 2000s were the devastation left after the tech bubble burst. These tsunamis of volatility occurred because of massive market dislocations, a fundamental swing and the end of a business cycle. However, for many of the smaller pullbacks over the past 40 years, there is no coincident fundamental trend. Much of the volatility in the market represents noise that is irrelevant to the economic bedrock and fundamental landscape for equities.

An extreme example of equity market noise occurred in 1987 on Black Monday, when the stock market experienced its worst day to date, losing over 20% of its value. Black Monday occurred as a result of numerous interconnected causes that led to an intense global sell-off. Remarkably, the market finished the year up 2% because, despite the volatility, economic growth continued and equity market fundamentals remained intact. Investors with the fortitude to stay invested through Black Monday would have experienced a positive return in 1987.

Frequent pullbacks in the market can be unsettling, and can encourage market timing, but investors should not jump ship. Being fully invested is particularly important when there is market volatility, because the best and the worst days in the market tend to be clustered together. If you were lucky enough to miss the worst days, you also were likely to have missed the best days.

Examining your quarterly statement, it is difficult to synthesize the portfolio impact of missing the best days in the market. However, Exhibit 4 shows that missing these days has a real impact on investment performance. A fully invested portfolio would have returned nearly double one that missed the 10 best days in the market. Additionally, as the majority of the best days occur within two weeks of the 10 worst days in the market, it is likely that investors who sold equity because of seasickness after a bad day often also missed a big rebound.

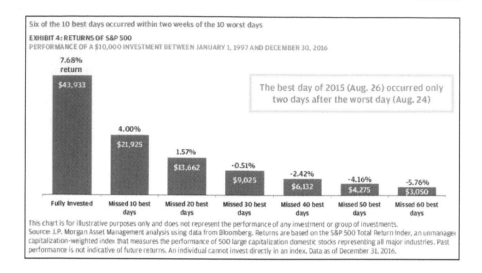

Six of the 10 best days occurred within two weeks of the 10 worst days

EXHIBIT 4: RETURNS OF S&P 500
PERFORMANCE OF A $10,000 INVESTMENT BETWEEN JANUARY 1, 1997 AND DECEMBER 30, 2016

7.68% return
$43,933

The best day of 2015 (Aug. 26) occurred only two days after the worst day (Aug. 24)

4.00%
$21,925

1.57%
$13,662

-0.51%
$9,025

-2.42%
$6,132

-4.16%
$4,275

-5.76%
$3,050

| Fully Invested | Missed 10 best days | Missed 20 best days | Missed 30 best days | Missed 40 best days | Missed 50 best days | Missed 60 best days |

This chart is for illustrative purposes only and does not represent the performance of any investment or group of investments. Source: J.P. Morgan Asset Management analysis using data from Bloomberg. Returns are based on the S&P 500 Total Return Index, an unmanaged capitalization-weighted index that measures the performance of 500 large capitalization domestic stocks representing all major industries. Past performance is not indicative of future returns. An individual cannot invest directly in an index. Data as of December 31, 2016.

3. Focus on the destination: Investors with a long time horizon experience less volatile returns.

While volatility can cause major deviations in the near term for equity markets, investors should focus on their destination. Examining rolling returns for equities in Exhibit 5 shows that, while historic annual returns have varied from -38% to +47% in a single year, rolling annualized returns, over a 20-year period, have been positive for the past 60 years.

Unfortunately, short-term investors are much more likely to realize the waves of volatility that occur over the one-year investment horizon. Investors with long-term goals, who are able to shift their focus to the long-term return potential of equity investments, have the luxury of realizing infrequent negative equity market returns.

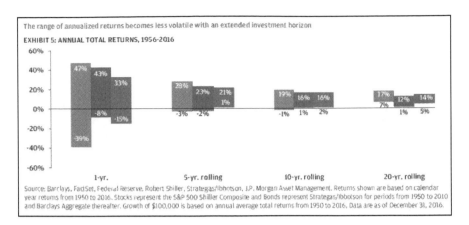

The range of annualized returns becomes less volatile with an extended investment horizon

EXHIBIT 5: ANNUAL TOTAL RETURNS, 1956-2016

Source: Barclays, FactSet, Federal Reserve, Robert Shiller, Strategas/Ibbotson, J.P. Morgan Asset Management. Returns shown are based on calendar year returns from 1950 to 2016. Stocks represent the S&P 500 Shiller Composite and Bonds represent Strategas/Ibbotson for periods from 1950 to 2010 and Barclays Aggregate thereafter. Growth of $100,000 is based on annual average total returns from 1950 to 2016. Data are as of December 31, 2016.

4. Batten down the hatches with diversification.

We live in a headline-driven world, where media often impacts equity prices in the near term. But your portfolio should not be a dinghy tossed and turned by market churn; it is possible to gain portfolio stability through diversification. While equities tend to perform better with economic growth and moderate levels of inflation, rate-sensitive fixed income is important to portfolios when economic growth falters. Although we have a positive outlook on U.S. equities in the coming year, other developed market equities can give your portfolio both exposure to risk factors outside the U.S. economy and to faster-growing emerging market economies that may help boost portfolio returns. Small cap stocks provide a pro-cyclical tilt to a portfolio compared to large cap stocks, though they can also be more sensitive to growth scares.

While a combination of various asset classes should improve portfolio returns, diversification is most valuable for keeping a portfolio on an even keel. Exhibit 6 illustrates how diversification has improved the risk/return profile of an asset allocation portfolio relative to equities over the past 20 years. This means investors in a diversified asset allocation portfolio cruised past market volatility feeling the fewest waves possible. A key to achieving more portfolio stability is to batten down the hatches with diversification before a storm hits.

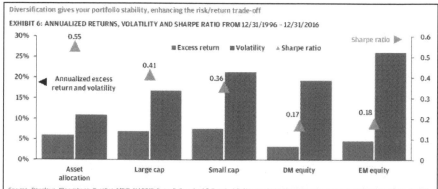

Diversification gives your portfolio stability, enhancing the risk/return trade-off

EXHIBIT 6: ANNUALIZED RETURNS, VOLATILITY AND SHARPE RATIO FROM 12/31/1996 - 12/31/2016

Source: Barclays, Bloomberg, FactSet, MSCI, NAREIT, Russell, Standard & Poor's, J.P. Morgan Asset Management. Large cap: S&P 500, Small cap: Russell 2000, EM Equity: MSCI EME, DM Equity: MSCI EAFE, The "Asset Allocation" portfolio assumes the following weights: 25% in the S&P 500, 10% in the Russell 2000, 15% in the MSCI EAFE, 5% in the MSCI EME, 25% in the Barclays Aggregate, 5% in the Barclays 1-3m Treasury, 5% in the Barclays Global High Yield Index, 5% in the Bloomberg Commodity Index and 5% in the NAREIT Equity REIT Index. Balanced portfolio assumes annual rebalancing. Annualized (Ann.) return and volatility (Vol.) represents period of 12/31/96 - 12/31/16. All data represent total return for stated period. Excess return is calculated using the Barclays 1-3m Treasury as a proxy for the risk-free rate. Data are as of December 31, 2016.

Navigating volatility

Though it is impossible to predict the future, expecting market volatility in the coming years is a safe bet. Just as the last 20 years have favored the diversified investor, we expect the next 20 years to do the same. Investors need risk assets in their portfolios to reach long-term investment goals, and staying invested throughout that time horizon can be investors' biggest challenge. History shows that diversification and rebalancing are the best tools for reducing portfolio volatility and providing a gentler ride through sometimes difficult seas.

Isaac Newton was a genius, but even he lost millions in the stock market

Elena Holodny, *Business Insider* (Apr. 20, 2017)

Isaac Newton was one of the smartest people to ever live. But being a smart physicist is not necessarily the same thing as being a smart investor. And, unfortunately for him, Newton learned that the hard way.

In an updated and annotated text of Benjamin Graham's classic "The Intelligent Investor," WSJ's Jason Zweig included an anecdote about Newton's adventures investing in the South Sea Company:

> "Back in the spring of 1720, Sir Isaac Newton owned shares in the South Sea Company, the hottest stock in England. Sensing that the market was getting out of hand, the great physicist muttered that he 'could calculate the motions of the heavenly bodies, but not the madness of the people.' Newton dumped his South Sea shares, pocketing a 100% profit totaling £7,000. But just months later, swept up in the wild enthusiasm of the market, Newton jumped back in at a much higher price — and lost £20,000 (or more than $3 million in [2002-2003's] money. For the rest of his life, he forbade anyone to speak the words 'South Sea' in his presence."

Here's a look at how South Seas moved back then.

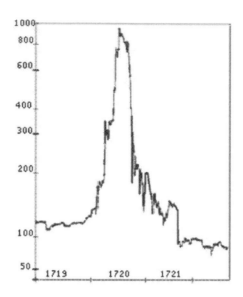

Newton obviously wasn't an unintelligent person. He invented calculus and conceptualized his three laws of motion. But this little episode shows that he wasn't a smart investor because he let his emotions get the best of him, and got swayed by the irrationality of the crowd.

Or as Graham described it: "For indeed, the investor's chief problem — and even his worst enemy — is likely to be himself."

Complexity Is More Appealing Than Simplicity: The 4 Reasons

1. It's Interesting

What sounds more stimulating as an allocator of capital? Traveling to New York, Silicon Valley and London for due diligence trips to meet with hedge fund, private equity and venture capital managers; getting wined and dined with free food and booze while getting to hear about complicated strategies, alpha, new technologies and 'what sets us apart' in an effort to beat the market and your peers. Or choosing a sensible asset allocation, keeping costs low, staying operationally efficient, avoiding crippling mistakes, setting reasonable goals and doing nothing most the of time. It's obvious why the majority of large investors choose the first option, but that doesn't mean these funds will be better off financially from this decision.

2. They Think It's Their Job to Outperform

Most institutional investors assume their job is to outperform the markets and their benchmarks to earn their keep (and most likely a performance bonus). Most board members are also very successful in business, ultra-competitive and want nothing more than to beat the performance numbers from endowments like Harvard and Yale. But it's not enough to beat their peers. Many also have to somehow prove their intellectual superiority by making their portfolios and strategies so opaque that most people within the organization have no idea how the money is actually being managed. It's an ego contest. Everyone wants to beat everyone else even with different goals and somehow complexity becomes the norm.

3. They Assume Complex Must be Better

The investors that run complex portfolios are highly educated individuals who are very intelligent. It can be hard for them to admit that a simpler solution makes the most sense. There is a false sense of security in doing what everyone else is doing. The assumption is that complex financial markets require complex solutions, but new and exciting is not the same thing as useful.

4. Social Validation

Psychologist Robert Cialdini has shown that one of the main filters we use to make decisions is by looking at the decisions of others. Social proof is the idea that it feels more comfortable to go along with the crowd when making tough decisions because we look at what others are doing in times of uncertainty. Investors with lots of money at stake tend to feel that they have to use "sophisticated" investment strategies that cost a lot of money in order to keep up with their peers. I've seen complexity fail over multiple investment cycles in these types of portfolios, but as Keynes told us, "Worldly wisdom teaches that it is better for the reputation to fail conventionally than to succeed unconventionally." Simplicity has become the exception, while complexity is now the rule.

People confuse simple with easy and complex with sophisticated. It's easier to sell complex strategies and ideas. Complexity leads to a false sense of job security under the guise of expert status, black box strategies or intellectual superiority. Complexity is a wonderful sales technique because it makes you seem indispensable.

Nassim Taleb covered the idea of complexity versus simplicity in his book, *Antifragile*:

> "A complex system, contrary to what people believe, does not require complicated systems and

regulations and intricate policies. The simpler, the better. Complications lead to multiplicative chains of unanticipated effects. [. . .] Yet simplicity has been difficult to implement in modern life because it is against the spirit of a certain brand of people who seek sophistication so they can justify their profession".

Here are some of the unanticipated effects of defaulting to a complex investment strategy:

- Fewer people understand what they're actually investing in so at the first sign of trouble they panic or have no idea how to react.

- Investors change strategies more often because they had no overarching philosophy to begin with.

- It becomes easier to get swindled by scams or buy into false claims by professional investors or consultants who are more adept at selling than investing.

- Investors are willing to pay a charisma premium simply because a portfolio manager or firm give off the aura of intellectual superiority.

- People assume that they will be awarded points for degree of difficulty in the markets.

In many ways, a simpler approach to investing is more challenging than a complex approach because simple can be harder to adhere to. Simple doesn't make for a compelling sales pitch. It's not sexy. No one brags about simplifying their investment strategy to their peers. People assume simple means simplistic.

Ten Bear Market Truths

1. Stock prices often decline. Half of all years since 1950 have seen a double-digit correction in stocks. Expect it.

2. They're a natural outcome of a complex trading and valuation system called the Market Mechanism—which is responsive to emotions and strongly held divergent opinions.

3. Everyone says bear markets are healthy until they actually happen. Then bear markets seem scary and investors who were looking for a better entry point begin to panic.

4. The majority of the people who have been scaring investors by predicting a bear market every single month for the past seven years will be the last ones to put their money to work when one actually hits.

5. It's an arbitrary number. I have no idea why everyone decided that a 20% loss constitutes a bear market. The media will pay a lot of attention to this definition while it doesn't matter at all to investors. The 1990s saw zero 20% corrections but two 19% drawdowns. Stocks also lost 19% in 2011. Does that extra 1% really matter?

6. Buy and hold feels great during a long bull market. It only works as a strategy if you continue to buy and hold when stocks fall. Both are much easier to do when stocks rise.

7. Your favorite pundit isn't going to be able to help you make it through the next one. Perspective and context can help, but there's nothing that can prepare an investor for the gut-punch you feel when seeing a chunk of your portfolio fall in value.

8. History is a broad outline of what can happen in the markets,

not what will happen. Every cycle is different.

9. They're very difficult to predict. All of the valuations, fundamentals, technicals and sentiment data in the world won't help you predict when or why investors decide it's time to panic.

10. These are the times that successful investors separate themselves from the pack. Most investors mistakenly assume that you make all of your money during bull markets. The reason so many investors fail is because they make poor decisions when markets fall.

History of Bear Markets of the Past 50 Years

Decline	Average Frequency	Average Length
5% or more	3 times a year	47 days
10% or more	Once a year	115 days
15% or more	Once every 2 years	216 days
20% or more	Once every 3.5 years	338 days

Source: Grayeli

Bull Markets vs. Bear Markets

In a bull market you're not as smart as you think you are—and in a bear market you're not as dumb as you think you are.

Bull Markets	Bear Markets
Fear of missing out.	Fear of being in.
Everything I buy is going up—I'm a genius.	Everything I buy is going down—I'm an idiot.
See, fundamentals always win out.	See, technicals and sentiment rule the markets.
I knew I should have had more of my portfolio in stocks.	I knew I should have had more of my portfolio in bonds.
That guy's been calling for a crash for years–he's an idiot.	That guy just called the crash–he's a genius.
I want to be a long-term buy and hold investor.	I want to be a short-term trader.
I'm glad I was buying during the last market crash.	Never try to catch a falling knife.
I'll sit tight when the market falls.	Dear Lord, get me out of stocks NOW!
Time to buy stocks?	Time to sell stocks"
Warren Buffett is washed up.	Wait, Buffett is buying here?
Buy & hold works.	Buy & hold is dead.
I'll be greedy when others are fearful.	I lied--I'm fearful when others are fearful.
Buy the dip.	Sell the rip.
Why didn't I invest earlier in my life?	I'll never invest again.
Why should I want to diversify?	Why was I so concentrated?
I'm just waiting for a healthy correction to put more money to work.	This market action is not healthy at all.
Don't worry, we'll outperform during the next downturn.	Don't worry, we'll outperform when the market turns around.
It feels like markets will never fall again.	It feels like markets will never rise again.

This table shows the various emotional states and rationalizations investors tend to go through during bull and bear markets. As you can see, for each reaction there is a corresponding one that represents the same error in the other context.

The First Totally Honest Stock Market Story

This article, first published in *The Wall Street Journal*, has become a classic of investment literature. The text is a bit small and faded in parts, but it is well worth the read.

The First Totally Honest Stock Market Story

FRIDAY'S MARKETS

By VINNIE FOSTER WYNANS III
Staff Reporter of THE WALL STREET JOURNAL

The market rallied early this morning for reasons nobody understands and nobody predicted. CNBC analysts confidently asserted it had something to do with the Senegalese money supply, but others pointed to revised monthly figures showing a poor tuna haul off the Peruvian coast.

The Dow turned down in late morning due to profit-taking—which is a meaningless phrase we financial journalists use when we don't know what we are talking about.

Around noontime, the tech stocks rallied (perhaps a result of profit-giving?) before a late wave of selling sent stocks lower. (This wave of selling was miraculously met by a wave of buying since in each transaction there is one buyer and one seller.)

All in all, it was a normal day on Wall Street. Advances led declines by 4 to 1, the bond market was incomprehensibly boring, the Mets beat the Phillies 6 to 2, and Kate Winslet's measurements remained 35-29-38.

For the bulk of this story, as in most financial services stories, I will quote from a series of famous blowhards, all of whom predicted that this bull market would top out at 7500.

"Some of the young bucks think that markets only go up, and not down," opines Seymour Kaufman of Dean-Witter-Marcus-Garvey. "They've been misled by the experience of the past 17 years."

"Sure I've missed the last 6,000 points of the rally," says Sherman McCoy of First Swiss-Credit Boston, who shifted his assets into gold last spring. "but when the correction comes, my position is going to be looking pretty good."

"I thought the market was overvalued at 8000," says Chris Clough of Travelers-Citicorp-Disney-American-Express-Baskin-Robbins-Lynch & Jenrette. "Now that PE ratios are 67 times higher, my argument is more intellectually coherent than ever."

We journalists put these quotations into our stories to prove we are savvy old heads (even if we are 25-year-olds fresh from a wire service), but if you listen to any of the advice from these old goats you are crazy. In fact if you have read this far into the story, you are nuts too.

Professional traders will know all about yesterday's markets from their computer terminals, and they shouldn't need a $37,000 a year journalist to spin it out for them. Normal investors shouldn't read day-to-day market reports because it will only cause them to churn their accounts.

Elaine Garzarelli has to be mentioned in every market story so this is the paragraph in which I am doing that. "Past performance is no guarantee of future results," said Ms. Garzarelli sagely.

To fill out the rest of my space so I can go home I will now throw in a few company results, which you could read on the most active table if you were really interested. Microsoft was up 1/4. Dell was down 1/8. Motorola was down 2. Hi Mom. Exxon was up 3 1/8. If anybody would like a slightly used Exercycle, please call (212) 555-2000. Ford was up 1/2. Germany is invading Belgium. I see England, I see France, I see someone's underpants. Bloomberg was off by 2 1/2.

Late news flash: the Clinton administration has signed a new incentives package with the American people that allows the president to sexually assault a stewardess every time the Dow crosses another 1000 barrier.

Made in the USA
San Bernardino, CA
17 November 2017